CW00798807

THE EAST END BUTCHER

Joe Lawrence.

The writing of The East End Butcher Boy has been a journey. It's a story that I always wanted to write. But had to wait for the right time. That time has come.

It's a "true" story. But names, dates and locations have been changed for obvious reasons. It all happened a long time ago but some wounds never heal.

There are many people to thank. Matthew Marland for his help in editing. Tony Cook for his advice. My wife Jill for her love and support. Tom, Sophie, Leanne and Chrystal for helping along the way. Stuart, Colin and Ian, three mates who have listened to this story for years and my Mum for getting me the bloody job in the first place.

And, a special mention to two people who are sadly no longer with us. My Dad, who was always my inspiration and Ronny, a dearly loved and sadly lost good friend.

And of course ROY.

PREFACE

The World and Me in 1972

The World

The world was a strange place in 1972. It was trying hard to move on into the modern seventies but was always being dragged back into the sixties. I suppose it was somewhere between the two.

Edward Heath was Prime Minister and was desperately struggling to change things left over from the last decade. The trade unions were still all-powerful and Heath was determined to reign them in. His attempts to confront them resulted in the Miners strikes of 1972 and 1974, the latter of which resulted in much of the country's industry working a three day week to conserve energy. No coal meant no power.

So Heath called a general election hoping that the country would back him. It didn't. Harold Wilson became the new Prime Minister just as he had in 1964 and there we were again, right back in the sixties.

Music was unsure which direction to go in. We had Engelbert Humperdink, Cliff Richard, the New Seekers and the Partridge Family, all with hits that could just as easily have come out of a sixties chart. Yet the seventies were also producing Glam Rock, with T.Rex, Slade and The Sweet. But then there was Don Mclean and Harry Nilsson, who could have come from either decade. And there was Luxembourg. No, not the radio station, the country. Yes, little old Luxembourg won the Eurovision Song Contest.

Not far from where I lived, Fords were turning out Escorts and Cortina's, cars that looked like they belonged in the sixties. But they were also producing the Capri. Now this was definitely a modern car, a true seventies car. Everyone wanted a Ford Capri.

Then there was fashion. Men still dressed in a sixties style but were wearing their hair long. And, for the first time they were trying to smell nice. Old Spice, Brut and Hai Karate were all seen as the smell of the seventies, but were in fact all launched in the late sixties.

Women were unsure if they should still be wearing sixties mini-skirts or seventies trouser suits and long dresses. Designer labels were starting to arrive, and the buzz words were Adidas, Ben Sherman, Brutus, Pierre Cardin and Laura Ashley.

It was the same at the cinema. The hit sixties TV show Steptoe and Son was made into a feature length film and came out at the same time as Carry on Matron. But in Soho they were daring to show Last Tango in Paris and Deep Throat. In America they had just released The Godfather.

In sport, the Winter Olympics was held in Sapporo, and true to form, England didn't win a single medal. Jack Bodell was once again British Heavyweight Champion, just as he had been back in 1969. Derby County under Brian Clough won the old First Division Championship and Leeds United won the FA Cup in May.

Elsewhere in the world, Nixon made a surprise visit to China, Ceylon decided to call itself Sri Lanka, RMS Queen Elizabeth was destroyed by fire in Hong Kong harbour and five White House operatives were arrested for burglary in something that was being called the Watergate scandal.

As I said, it was a strange old world back in 1972.

Me

In March 1972, I was fourteen years old and living on a council estate in East London with Mum, Dad and Sister Ruth. We weren't poor but we certainly weren't rich either. Dad worked at the local gas works as a boilermaker's mate (whatever that meant) and was paid seventeen pounds per week.

The London Docks were pretty much closed by then, which meant there were just two main places of work in our area. Fords in Dagenham or Becton Gas Works in East Ham. Dad had tried Fords a few years earlier but the shift work got him down. So he decided to leave and work at Becton. Dad was a grafter. It was hard, dirty work. He would come home late at night covered in coal dust, but he never complained, just got on with it.

Dad was one of six. He had a brother and four sisters, and on my Dad's side I had eight cousins. Dad's parents had moved to Dagenham just before the war from Bermondsey in South East London. They were a hard, tough, boxing family with a fierce reputation. They were the sort of family that you didn't mess with.

Mum was a dinner lady at the local school, but not mine, which was a shame because I could have done with the extra rations. In 1972 she was almost forty, still a stunner and a great mum. She was always there when we went to school and always there when we got home.

Food was on the table at six every night and she could always make something out of nothing. Not that she often had to, there was always a lot left over from the school dinners. We ate well and so did our dog, a mongrel called Pete. We bought Pete as an eight week old pup from an Irish family who lived in the next street. My Dad took one look at him and said "Look at the size of his paws, he's gonna be a big dog." He was convinced that you could tell how big a dog was going to be by the size of their paws as a pup.

Dad was wrong. Pete grew up to be the size of a Corgi but with enormous paws!

My sister, Ruth, was three years older than me. She'd left school and was training to be a nursery nurse. She went to college in London but also had a Saturday job in Bartons, the local bakers. This meant that we got lots of free bread and cakes. Whatever was left in the shop when it closed on Saturday was given to the staff to take home. Some weeks Ruth had so many boxes to carry that Dad would have to bring her home in the car. We became very popular with the neighbours at weekends.

Me, I was a cocky little teenager, a bit scrawny but good looking. With blonde hair and blue eyes, the girls loved me and I just loved the girls! I had a bit of the "David Cassidy" look going on. My hair was shoulder length and I would spend hours blow drying it so that my centre parting stood up each side. The "David Cassidy" look was very important for attracting the girls in 1972.

Now although I may have looked a bit like David Cassidy, I couldn't stand his music. I was listening to Al Green, Curtis Mayfield, The O'Jays, Stevie Wonder and Harold Melvin. Oh yes, I was a soul boy. Strange really, since though my taste in music was very black, my fashion was very much "white boy". Ben Sherman's, two - tone tonic trousers and Solatio shoes. If you weren't wearing this kind of gear in my area you were nobody.

So, imagine a young teenage boy with long blonde hair like David Cassidy, but dressed as a "skin head". That was me…

At fourteen, I was slight of build, and my nickname was tin ribs. Although I played rugby, it was for my speed, not my size. I was beginning to find my feet in the world, always up to mischief but never anything heavy. I loved a scrap - what fourteen year old boy doesn't - but in those days it was all fisticuffs and nothing more. I stole from Woolworths (just because everyone else did), had a bit of a cocky attitude, and would talk back to Mum, but never Dad.

Dad never laid a hand on me but his word was law. He could give me a look that would reduce me to tears within seconds and that remained the same until the day he died and by that time I was forty eight.

We'd never been out of the country on holiday. Back then there were no day trips to France or holidays to Spain. Holidays for us were an Aunt's caravan in Dovercourt, Essex. It was less than seventy miles away, but in those days it could take practically a whole day to get there. Dad drove a Ford Corsair (DYU 697C). It's strange how I can still remember the number plate after all these years.

Our house was quite big by most council house standards. It had three bedrooms and a downstairs toilet as well as a bathroom and a toilet upstairs. We had moved five years earlier from a two-up two-down old house on the other side of town. That house had no inside toilet or bathroom - the toilet was out in the garden which was fine during the day, but at night and in the winter, was a nightmare. So we used a pot at night that we kept under the bed. We kept a tin bath outside in the garden and on a Friday night Dad would bring it into the kitchen so we could all have a bath. We took turns but all used the same water. Being the youngest I went last, and to be honest, I'm not sure how much cleaner I came out afterwards. The only tap in the house was in the kitchen and that was just cold water. But we did have an "Ascot" that provided us with a small amount of hot water. The kitchen sink was where everyone washed every day and priority was always given to Dad so he could have his morning shave there.

We used to joke that they were pulling it down to build a slum. As it turned out, they built a series of high rise blocks of flats. Mum and Dad were offered one of these but stuck to their guns and refused to move until they were offered a house. Everyone else in the street moved into the high rises, and it wasn't long before we were the only family left in our street. It was horrible for a few months. There were over forty small houses in our road and they were all derelict apart from ours. You can imagine the number of rats and mice that were running around everywhere. The council thought we would give in, but they hadn't bargained for my Dad, who just wouldn't be beat.

Then one day they got the offer they were waiting for, a nice three bedroom house on the best kept council estate in the area. It was what they had both dreamed of. We moved in two weeks later.

As the years went on the joke about out old house being pulled down to build a slum proved to be true, as the new estate that was built there, now has one of the worst reputations in the whole of East London.

So, my life was all good at fourteen. It was stable. I had good parents, and was doing reasonably well at school (but no genius).

Little did I know that this year would be a turning point in my life and open my eyes to a whole new world. It would also be the start of one massive adventure that would ultimately shape my future.

Chapter 1.

Introductions

It was Saturday morning at 10.40am in March 1972. I was still in bed when I heard a sound that would send fear into any fourteen year old boy.

"It's about time you got yourself a Saturday job."

It was Mum shouting up the stairs. I took no notice and went back to sleep.

The following Saturday I was woken again by Mum's voice, but this time it struck much more fear into me than it had the week before.

"I think I've got you a job; get yourself down to Roy the Butcher cos he's looking for some help clearing up on Saturdays."

Mum had this thing about working. As soon as you reached fourteen in our house you had to start looking for a job. Not a real job of course, officially you couldn't leave school until you were sixteen. But a Saturday job. My sister got a Saturday job when she was fourteen at the local bakers, and she still had the job even though she was nearly seventeen and at college Monday till Friday.

And so on Saturday 14th March 1972 I set off to see Roy the Butcher. I knew the shop well. I had to pass it every-day on the way to school. But I'd never taken any notice of it. To me it was just another shop in a small parade of shops on a busy street. Mum said I had to be there at 11.00am, and since the shop was about twenty minutes' walk from our house, she made me leave at 10.30am. I decided to take my time. I figured that if I turned up late there was no chance of them taking me on. I was nervous, more nervous than I'd ever been in my life. But I kept telling myself that it was only an interview, and if I acted a bit dumb, I would never see them again. I wasn't sure what I expected, but it was work and that was never good.

I eventually arrived at the shop at 11.20.

The first thing I noticed was the smell. It was a mixture of sawdust, blood and raw meat, and for some unknown reason, I loved it. I don't know what it was about the smell but somehow I felt at home. There seemed to be a lot going on, there was activity everywhere, customers were talking, the butchers were talking and laughing, there was a radio on in the background pumping out music from Radio One. There was almost a party atmosphere. It was hard to take it all in.

There was meat everywhere, hanging from every available space. Legs of pork, bits of lamb, rolls of beef, rabbits hung up still with their fur on, even pig heads. It was fantastic; suddenly I was like a kid in a sweet shop.

It wasn't a big shop, but the way it was laid out made it seem smaller than it really was. This, as I learnt later, was all a con. As soon as there were five or six people in the shop it became crowded, and anyone else coming in had to start queuing outside. Passers-by would then assume that the shop must sell really good quality meat, because there was always a queue of people waiting to get in.

I was greeted by a lad of seventeen called Stevie. I recognised Stevie straightaway because he had gone to school with my sister Ruth, and I, funnily enough, had gone to school with his sister, Carol. He was skinny with long, blond, highlighted curly hair. He had one of those curly perms that for some reason men in the seventies (mainly footballers) thought looked really cool, but actually made them look like a complete twat. He looked at me and smiled, but he was also holding the biggest knife I had ever seen.

"Ah, you must be Joe. Roy, the new Saturday boy's here!"

From the back of the shop appeared Roy, over 6ft tall, with thick black hair and a large droopy moustache, the sort you see on a Mexican in an old cowboy film. He was in his mid- twenties, square jawed and a big muscular frame. He had a kind of aura about him. This was a man that once met was never forgotten. A big smile swept across his face and he shouted at me in a voice that seemed to boom and echo throughout the shop.

"You're fucking late, the kettle's out the back, now go and make us all a cup of tea, here's a quid, walk over to the bakers and get us a dozen doughnuts."

He laughed and then disappeared into one of the walk-in fridges.

I was stunned. I thought I was going for some kind of interview, instead I was now the new Saturday boy and working straightaway.

Stevie got me a white coat and a striped apron to wear. Both were far too big so the sleeves were rolled up and the apron folded over and somehow tied up. I put the kettle on and before I knew what was happening I was walking across the road towards the bakers to buy twelve doughnuts. I kept wondering who they were all for? Perhaps there were a lot more butchers working at the shop that I hadn't met yet.

I walked into the bakers. A large, buxom middle aged woman with red hair was standing behind the counter. She eyed me up and down, then started laughing.

"Dozen doughnuts love?"

"Yes please." I replied, wondering how she could possibly have known.

"You must be Roy's new Saturday boy. What's your name, love?"

"Err, yes, I am, Joe, thanks."

All the girls in the shop stopped what they were doing and turned to look at me. They nodded and smiled, and I nodded and smiled back. The red haired lady wished me luck and I returned to the shop with a big grin on my face. I felt like some kind of celebrity.

I put the doughnuts down on the large butchers block at the back of the shop.

"Right." said Stevie. "There's no sugar, cos we don't take sugar, so I guess that means that you don't take sugar either. We like it strong with just a small drop of milk. Tea's a must in this shop so every hour stop what you're doing and stick the kettle on."

"Okay," was just about all I could say, and started to make the tea.

Roy came over, his white coat heavily stained with blood and carrying a massive meat cleaver. He sat down on the block.

"Okay, four doughnuts each for now. We'll have a proper bite to eat a bit later."

All I kept thinking about was the four doughnuts. Did he really say four doughnuts each? I can't eat four doughnuts! And what was this about eating something *proper* later on?

What I didn't realise then was that all the work in the shop was manual and heavy. These guys were burning calories like it was going out of fashion. They started at 07.00 and finished at 16.00 on a Saturday, and for those nine hours they worked constantly.

Roy and Stevie drank their tea, ate their doughnuts in minutes and went straight back to work. They were either serving at the front of the shop, replacing the meat in the window or cutting up fresh joints. They were constantly on the move, and apart from drinking tea, they hardly ever stopped.

Everyone who came into the shop were known by their first name, and if in doubt the woman were called "darling" and the men were called "guvnor".

They cracked jokes with everyone, and were a bit risqué with the woman. There were lots of double meanings, if you know what I mean.

A young woman would come in and ask for a pound of sausages, and Stevie would say, "Good choice darling, you look like you could do with a nice sausage tonight!" Stevie would laugh, Roy would laugh, the young lady would laugh and everyone in the shop would laugh. No one took offense because it was all good clean fun. I felt as though I'd stepped into another world. A world that I was eager to be part of.

I carried on with my work, which included washing and scrubbing the cutting blocks, making sure the floors were kept clear so no one slipped up, and putting extra sawdust down when needed. In short, I was a general gofer.

At two o'clock, Roy gave me some money to get three bags of chips and six buttered rolls. It was the same as it had been in the bakers. The Greek man in the chip shop knew exactly what I wanted and gave me three of the biggest bags of chips I'd ever seen in my life. He also wished me luck and I walked back to the shop with a big smile on my face.

Although I was still full up from the doughnuts, I ate my two chip rolls, drank my tea and got back to work just like the others. The next few hours seem to fly by.

When 4 o'clock came and we were almost finished, I was completely knackered. I had never worked so hard in my life. But, surprisingly, I had loved it. It seemed like one big adventure.

Roy called me over and gave me three crisp one pound notes.

"There you go, son. I've paid you for a full day even though you only worked from half past eleven. Take a few pork chops home for your Dad's tea as well."

"Thanks, Roy."

Stevie went into the large walk-in fridge, came out with a bag and threw it at me. My arms were so tired I just about managed to catch it.

"There's your chops."

As Roy was closing down the shutters, he shouted out to me.

"Joe, don't forget, Saturdays we all start at seven, so see you then, don't be fucking late next week."

Seven? Did he really say seven? I had never seen seven o'clock in the morning. That would mean I would have to be up at 6.00 and leave by 06.30. Not quite sure I could do that.

Me and Stevie walked along together. He lived with his parents just a few minutes from the shop. He looked at me and smiled.

"Well, what did you think of your first day?"

"Hard work, but I enjoyed it and it went really quickly."

"He's a bit of a character, is Roy, but he looks after you if you work hard. There's a lot that goes on in the shop that you'll get involved in as time goes on. See you next Saturday, seven o'clock, don't be late, Roy hates anyone that's late. By the way, there's seven pork chops in the bag and a couple of pounds of rump steak. Make sure you eat well next week, we need to build you up a bit."

I walked the rest of the way home, gave Mum the bag of meat, sat in the armchair, fell asleep and woke up six hours later.

Chapter 2

Learning The Ropes

The following Saturday I was up at 06.00am and in the shop by 06.50. Roy and Stevie had already started to put the meat on display in the window. This was called "putting the window in."

Although it wasn't even seven o'clock, the whole place seemed to be alive with activity. As usual Radio One was pumping out loud pop music and Roy and Stevie were singing along as they worked. I couldn't believe people could be that lively at that time in the morning. Where on earth did these guys get their energy from?

My first job, as always, was to put the kettle on and make tea, then go over to the bakers and get some rolls. Roy's shop had a cold meat counter and Stevie sliced huge, thick slices of ham on the meat slicer. It was only just half past seven and we were already eating huge ham rolls and drinking large mugs of tea.

Roy and his wife Sue lived above the shop in a two bedroom flat. He had started at 06.00 that morning and Stevie had got there around 06.30. Our break lasted no more than five minutes when Roy suddenly said, "Right, let's crack on, Stevie, tell Joe what to do, if he gets it wrong I'll bollock you, not him." Then he roared with laughter.

Stevie looked at me and said, without any humour what-so-ever, "Okay, I'll tell you everything once, if you get it wrong I'll tell you again, but there is never a third time, understand?"

 I nodded. "Yep, okay, I'm a quick learner."

I was given the offal to put on display on six steel trays. Each one had to be filled with different offal. There was lambs liver, lambs hearts, lambs tongues, lamb kidneys, ox liver and pig kidneys. Once these were filled, I had to put them in the right hand corner of the window. A simple job you may think, but Roy was a hard task master, and if he wasn't happy he was quick to let you know. He let me know VERY quickly.

"Look at the state of that offal; it looks like a fucking abortion!"

The sternness of his language made me freeze. I honestly thought he was going to thump me or at the very least, sack me. Instead he laughed out loud.

"Come here, wanker, let me show you how it's done."

He emptied the offal onto one of the blocks and then carefully put it back onto the different trays. He was right, as soon as he showed me how to arrange it properly, it made sense and looked a million times better.

I learnt very quickly that presentation was everything to Roy. His window display had to be perfect; there was no room for shoddy work.

Stevie took me to one side.

"Look, take no notice of the way Roy says things. He doesn't really mean it, it's just the way he is. He used to work down Smithfield Market, it's the way everyone talks down there."

"Okay Stevie, thanks."

I felt reassured. My dad swore all the time. It was common language in our house, but dad very rarely used the "c" word. Roy used it all the time.

My next job was to make mincemeat. Stevie showed me how to use the mincer. It was a formidable machine. Nowadays a boy of fourteen just wouldn't be allowed to use it. Especially since the electrics in the shop were completely out of date and needed renewing. Sparks would fly from the plug and it would glow red hot. But, I just got on with it. Roy gave me cuts of meat in a huge plastic bowl (which turned out to be a baby's bath!) and said, "Okay, mince that up."

The meat had to go through the mincer twice to have the desired effect and he also added a bit of ox heart to make it look nice and red. Roy made his own sausages and I was given the job of putting these onto different steel trays according to their flavour. There was pork, beef or spicy pork.

Roy and Stevie were doing the heavier stuff; Roy was hanging a whole pig in the window, high up. Stevie was cutting up whole lambs on one of the blocks and taking off the legs and shoulders, then hanging them in a line in the window. Roy walked into the fridge and came out with a piece of beef that was as tall as me and weighed twice as much, but it was on his shoulder and he was singing away as though it was as light as a feather.

He slammed it onto the block and told me it was a hind quarter of beef. Within minutes he had cut it into recognisable joints and then hung these in the window.

That first hour was manic, but by 08.00 the window display was done and the shop officially opened.

Roy and Stevie went outside to see what their hard work looked like and whether any minor adjustments were needed. Once they were satisfied, I was given the nod and once again the kettle was boiled.

Roy popped over the road and came back five minutes later. There was another butchers shop on the other side of the road about one hundred yards away. Roy liked to have a look at their display and compare the two. Our window display always had to be the best.

Customers would start to come in from about 08.15 onwards and would keep coming until about 2.00 in the afternoon. It was non-stop.

My job now was to re-stock the window as soon as it started to empty. So every ten or fifteen minutes I would be looking at the meat in the window, seeing which trays were going down and then replacing them as required.

So that was the routine. Roy and Stevie would be serving, I would be replacing the empty trays in the window, and making tea all the time. Doughnuts were bought and eaten around 11.00, chips and rolls were bought and eaten around 2.00 and we started to clear up between three and four o'clock.

We were a good team; I got paid my three pounds, given some steak for "Dad's tea" and went home. Once again, completely knackered.

Although it was all new to me, it felt as though I had been doing it my whole life. It just came naturally.

I had only known Roy and Stevie for a week but I felt as though I had known them for years. In fact, they felt like older brothers, especially Roy.

I had no idea that my education in the next few years would be completely taken over by this charismatic man.

Chapter 3

Backslang, Betting, Beer and Bones.

After four or five Saturdays I had my role off to a fine art. They no longer had to ask or tell me to do anything, I just did it automatically. Roy asked if I could also work after school on Tuesdays, Wednesdays and Fridays. I jumped at the chance. I could be in the shop by four o'clock and help clear up for the last two hours and still be home by 6.30. Roy promised to give me five pound per week if I worked after school and on Saturdays.

It worked well. I would turn up at the shop, start emptying the window, scrub the blocks, sweep up and, of course, put the kettle on.

On Tuesdays and Wednesdays we would be out of the shop by 5.45 but on Fridays we were much busier and might not finish until 6.30. I didn't care, I was with Stevie and Roy and that's all that mattered.

When I think back to those days now, I realise we were just kids really. Me, fourteen, Stevie seventeen and Roy only twenty five. We would play practical jokes on each other. (Well, mostly on me actually). I remember one day Stevie thought it would be hilarious to throw an egg at Roy; it hit him on the back of the head and exploded. That was it, Roy was off on one. He got half a dozen eggs and launched an attack on Stevie, and every one of them hit him on his head or neck, he was covered. Then for no reason at all they both thought it would be great fun to each throw a dozen eggs at me, but there was nowhere to run, so I got plastered.

Their other favourite joke was to send me on errands. These of course were all made-up. On one occasion Roy asked me to go to the butchers over the road to ask if we could borrow some instant water.

"We've run out of instant water Joe, run over the road and ask if we can borrow some, tell him its only for a couple of days and then I'll replace it."

"Okay Roy". I was off, running across to the other side of the road, only to be told by the other butchers, "No fucking way, he's not getting his instant water till we get our sky hooks back."

You can imagine the reception that greeted me when I returned and told Roy and Stevie what they had said. They both fell about laughing. It took a while but I soon got to understand their strange sense of humour.

Roy also taught me the butcher's back slang. This is a secret but very simple language that all butchers use. They could have whole conversations with each other and you would be convinced that it was a completely different language. It was invented by the old costermongers back in the eighteen hundreds and was quickly taken up by the butchery trade. Butchers could talk to each other and give instructions without the customers knowing what they were talking about. Every word is said backwards. It's where the word yob comes from, it's simply boy backwards.

So the word "old" becomes dlo. This is pronounced "deelow". The word "pork" is now krop, pronounced "kayrop". Lamb becomes "beemal".

A customer comes in and asks for a nice piece of lamb for the weekend. Roy then shouts to Stevie, "Stevie, get this nice lady that dlo bmal that's in the fridge." Stevie then knows to get the older piece of lamb and not the freshest.

Swearing was the best. You could call people the worst names and they had no idea! Bastard was dratsab, fuck was kaycuf and cunt was teenuc.

If someone came in that one of us didn't like and asked for a leg of pork we would call out "Get this dlo dratsab a nice dlo gel of krop". Great fun!

After six weeks, Stevie asked Roy if he could show me how to cut up a whole lamb. Roy agreed, but said it would have to be in our own time when the shop closed. So, at the end of the day when the shop was closed up, Stevie showed me where to cut and what to cut with (chopper, saw or knife) and then how to present it. He only showed me once and I had it. Soon I would be beating both Roy and Stevie in races to see who was the fastest.

One thing that I noticed very quickly about Roy was his obsession with waste. Everything had to be used.

"Waste is where my profit is." Was something he was always saying.

Any small off cuts of beef were used in mincemeat or beefburgers. Pork and lamb off cuts were put into sausages. Any offal that became "out of date" were bagged up and sold cheaply to the customers for dog food.

Most fats were minced then rendered down in a large gas "copper" in the yard at the back of the shop, put into small greaseproof containers and sold as dripping.

All bones were put into large sacks and sold to the "Boneman" once a week. He came round in a big 7.5t lorry, weighed the sacks and then paid Roy a few pence per pound for them.

Roy had a habit of checking the bones before the "Boneman" came to make sure they were clean. If he found any excess meat on them he would go mad at Stevie.

One week there were a few big beef bones that Roy managed to scrape an extra 6oz of meat off of. He weighed it and worked out was it was worth as mincemeat.

"I'm gonna deduct that from your fucking wages Stevie"

And he did. It was just a few pence but true to his word when Saturday came he took 10p out of Stevie's wages.

The more time I spent with Roy, the more I realised what a big gambler he was. He would bet on anything, but he especially liked the horses and the dogs. He bet all day, every day.

There was a betting shop on the parade across the road and Roy would be forever going backwards and forwards to get his bets on, especially on a Saturday afternoon.

One Saturday Roy took me aside.

"Come with me son, let me introduce you to some people."

We walked across the road to the betting shop. Roy went in and I waited outside. Even I knew you couldn't go into a betting shop until you were eighteen. He came out again.

"Come on, what the fuck you waiting for?"

We walked in. It was my first time in a betting shop, and it was full of men, smoke and noise. There was a loud speaker calling out names of horses and their odds. On one wall was a massive blackboard, and a man was listening to the loud speaker and then writing the odds down on the board. Roy took me up to the counter. Standing behind it were two flat nosed men looking rather menacing.

"Alfie, Chris, this is Joe, he's my new Saturday Boy. He'll be putting my bets on from time to time. Okay?"

The two guys behind the counter smiled and said "No problem, Roy."

From that day on I was Roy's runner.

The same went for the local pub which was across the road and opposite the shop. One Saturday while we were eating our chips and rolls, Roy asked Stevie if he fancied a pint. Stevie agreed.

"Joe, go over the pub and get us three pints of lager."

I thought it was just another wind up, so I just smiled and continued eating. Roy looked at me, put his hand in his pocket and pulled out a pound note.

"I'm serious, here's the money, go and get three pints."

"Roy, they won't serve me, I'm only fourteen."

"Just tell them it's for Roy the Butcher, it'll be fine."

I walked over to the pub, dressed in my white coat and striped apron, went up to the bar and very timidly said "Three pints of bitter, please", then added very quickly, "They're for Roy the Butcher."

The bar tender smiled and started to pull the pints. He put them on a tray and refused to take any money.

"Tell Roy, they're on me."

Within a few minutes I was back in the shop, drinking a pint of beer and eating chip rolls.

I felt like a proper grown up...

Chapter 4

Swags and Certificates

After a few more weeks of hard graft, Stevie took me aside and told me he had a "special" job for me.

"Okay Joe, you've been here a while now and me and Roy think it's time we gave you some extra responsibility."

I was chuffed. Little old me, only fourteen and being given a "special" job to do.

"Yeah sure Stevie, what is it?"

"The most important job in the shop, a job that we've all done, but have decided is now yours."

I could see Roy out of the corner of my eye; he was standing by one of the butcher blocks and was trying not to laugh.

"Hold on a minute Stevie, is this a wind up?"

Roy came over, still sniggering.

"Joe, we are entrusting this "special" job to you, do it well every Saturday and there will be an extra pound in your wages."

Roy had said the magic words "extra pound". Now I was definitely up for it.

"Okay, so what is it?"

They both looked at each other and then said one word in unison.

"SWAGS"

Now, swags is the slang word that all butchers use for sausages.

They both cracked up laughing. I didn't see what was funny; I already put the sausages on silver trays every Saturday for the window display.

"I don't get it, what's so funny? I already do the sausages."

Roy calmed himself and then very slowly said,

"Yes, Joe and you do a very good job, but from now on we also want you to make the little fuckers."

I was in shock. Make the sausages? The sausage machine was the biggest piece of machinery in the shop, it weighed a ton, and it was almost as tall as I was. But the thought of the extra pound was overwhelming.

"I'm up for it, just show me what to do and I'll make the best sausages ever."

Now, Roy had a saying, which he must have said to me fifty times during the first six weeks. He said it so often that it had become a standing joke, and as soon as he started to say it, me and Stevie would finish it off for him.

"Okay, I'll show you once, I'll even show you twice, but…"

Me and Stevie finished his sentence together.

"I'll never show you three times!"

Roy and Stevie then set about boning some pig heads and pork bellies until they had a large bowl full of pork.

"Okay Joe, every week me and Stevie will give you this amount of meat in this bowl. What you need to do is put this lot through the mincer."

Now that, I could do. From day one I had been making mincemeat for the window display, so the large industrial mincer held no fear for me. I put the pork into the big tray on top of the mincer and fed it through the machine back into the baby's bath. I now had minced pork.

Roy and Stevie looked pleased; Roy gave me a pat on the back.

"Well done son, part one completed. Now for the secret ingredients."

In the large walk-in fridge we kept a sack of rusk, like a dried breadcrumb, and inside the sack was a pint sized metal tankard.

"Okay, you need to add four jugs of rusk to the minced pork."

That was easy; I quickly put the rusk with the pork.

Roy then went and came back with four packets of Paxo stuffing from the window display.

"Okay, now add these to the mix."

I'd always wondered why we kept so much Paxo stuffing in the shop; there were cases of it everywhere but we only seemed to sell a few packets every week. Nevertheless, I did as I was told.

Roy then pulled out a large brown box from under one of the cooked meat counters. Inside the box were small white sachets. The only words on these packets were "Oriental Spices".

"You need to add one and a half of these into the mix and then four jugs of cold water."

This was easy so far; I did it and stood back. The smell of the spices was not unpleasant, but it did have the effect of making your eyes water.

"Now mix the whole lot up with your hands until it's mixed evenly."

This was harder than it looked and took a good ten minutes. I then had a very strange looking, but lovely smelling, swag mix.

"Right, put that back into the fridge and let it firm up for thirty minutes then put the whole thing through the mincer again, and when you've done that, then the fun begins."

We all went about our normal jobs. Half an hour later, I removed the mixture from the fridge and put it back through the mincer. It didn't go through as quickly or as easily as fresh meat did, but eventually I was ready.

"Okay Roy, I'm ready."

Roy came over and told me to push the sausage machine into the middle of the cutting room. Luckily it was on casters, but it was still very heavy. It was about five feet high and looked like a tall and lumpy chimney with a funnel coming out of it about halfway down and a large handle on one side; in fact, it looked like something out of Doctor Who.

Roy showed me how to unscrew the top and then told me to put as much of the sausage mixture as I could into the machine. I did it by hand and it took about twenty large handfuls. I screwed the top back on.

"Okay, now for the skins."

Roy went into the fridge and brought out a plastic container about twelve inches square. He took off the lid. Inside, swimming in salt water, were pig's intestines; they looked like thick pieces of pure white string.

"Now, take one of these and slide it over the funnel."

I did it. I was amazed at how long one of these things was. It seemed to take forever, it was about twelve feet long, but concertinaed up on the funnel to about ten inches.

"Now turn the handle and the mix will come out of the funnel. As it does, feed the skin onto it. Once you get started the skin will automatically grip the mix."

I turned the handle, and within a few seconds the mix came out of the funnel. I fed the skin onto it and kept turning the handle with one hand and guided the long skin with the other.

Roy watched me until all twelve feet of skin was full of sausage meat.

"Now comes the good bit, tying them into perfect size sausages. Go and get a sausage from the window display."

I took one from the window, and gave it to Roy.

"See the size of this? Every sausage you make has to be this size. If they are, that means there will be eight to the pound, and that's what people want, no more, no less."

Roy then picked up the long length of sausage from the bowl, his hands moving like lightening, twisting and turning, and suddenly he was holding four feet of sausages, all the perfect size and in bunches of three. He had suddenly become a magician.

"Okay, put another skin on and make another load, then it's your turn to do the tying."

I did as I was told and within five minutes there was another ten foot sausage in the bowl. Roy took his time and showed me how to tie them. I made a mess of the first few but in five minutes I had it. I was making sausages.

"Right, you've got it, now finish off this load and then wash the machine down with boiling water. From now on this will be your job every Saturday. A soon as the window is in get to work on the swags."

I realised why Stevie and Roy hated making sausages, it was messy and time consuming. But, for some strange reason I loved it.

From then on there was no stopping me. I became obsessed with them. I suggested new flavours to Roy, and he never said no, just told me to get on with it.

After two months I was making, pork, spicy pork, beef and horseradish, pork and cider, pork and apple, chilly beef, in fact anything I could think of. I even tried pork and orange which was a complete disaster. Not only was the taste vile but I'd forgotten about the pips!

The recipe basically remained the same, meat, rusk, paxo, but then I would add different flavourings like chilli flakes or horseradish. I would add cider instead of water. If I wanted to buy anything I would ask Roy and he would give me the money out of the till. We soon became well known in East London for our sausages.

I arrived at the shop one Saturday morning to find an envelope on one of the blocks with my name on it. I opened it, inside was a certificate and a ten pound note.

The certificate read, "The Annual Smithfield Sausage Competition. R Marshall Family Butchers, fourth place."

I was confused; I looked up at Roy and shrugged my shoulders.

"What's this then?"

"I took some of your sausages up to Smithfield for the annual competition, it's a big thing in the butchery game. This year over four hundred shops entered, and you, you little bastard, came fucking fourth!"

He and Stevie started clapping their hands and cheering. I was chuffed, and didn't know what to say.

"The tenner's yours, that's from me, now let's get to work, we're running late."

Roy walked away and got on with cutting up some lambs for the window.

I felt like a celebrity and I was ten quid richer. God, I loved making those swags.

Chapter 5.

Roy's Story

It was at this stage that I realised that by using Roy's name in this area, you could get anything you wanted. I was curious to find out why.

Roy Marshall was brought up in Bethnal Green in London's East End, with two brothers and a sister. His dad was a part time wrestler who later went on to fight "Big Daddy" and "Mick McManus." His mum was a cleaner at the local school.

He left school at sixteen with no qualifications and got a job in Smithfield Market with his school mate Mark.

Roy had always been a bit of a rogue at school. Bethnal Green was a tough area in the 1960's. He got into some minor criminal activity, but nothing serious.

Once he started down the market he was in his element. This was a time when security in Smithfield was almost non-existent. They had their own Market Police, but these were few and far between. Everyone was making a bit of money on the side. Some people were earning a fortune.

Roy started as a "cutter." Basically, he would cut up English lambs for a wholesaler in the market, the meat would then be taken to the scales to be weighed, and this would be checked by a "checker". The checker would write out a "ticket" (a kind of invoice), the buyer would take the ticket to the sales desk and hand it over to the cashier. The cashier would work out what was owed and the customer would pay. The buyer or customer would then get a market porter to carry the meat to his van. That's the way the system worked in those days.

Now this system was easy to make money out of if you were a certain kind of person, and Roy was most definitely that kind of person.

As a cutter, what you needed was a checker who was in on the scam and a customer who also wanted to make some money. Now most butchers are always up for making a quid or two, so finding customers was not a problem. At the wholesaler where Roy worked, the checker just happened to be Mark, Roy's old school mate.

So the scam began. For example, a customer would ask for twenty legs of lamb, Roy would cut them and put them on the scale. The actual weight would be 100lb, but Roy would shout to the checker that the weight was 78lb. The checker would look at the scale and agree. He would write out a ticket for 78lb at 35p per pound. The customer then takes the ticket to the sales desk and pays for 78lb at 35p. So he gets 22lb of lamb for free. He splits the difference with Roy and Mark and everyone's happy.

Some days the market was so busy and hectic that the checker may "forget" to write out a ticket for the goods and three or four whole lambs would be picked up by a porter and carried straight away to the butcher's van. There was always a way to make money.

It may not sound like a lot of money now, but Roy was only earning around £20 per week then. Most weeks the scam would give him and Mark another £60 each at least and some weeks it could run into hundreds of pounds.

Whilst he was working at Smithfield, Roy put himself on a two year butchery course (two evenings a week) at Smithfield College.

Roy worked in Smithfield for four years and was shrewd enough to save his scam money. Mark did the same but decided to go in another direction. Years later he had an enormous abattoir and wholesalers in East London and became a millionaire.

Don't get me wrong, Roy enjoyed himself, but he was very focused; he knew what he wanted to do. He had a dream of having a chain of butcher's shops all over the East End. By the time he was twenty he had enough saved to buy his own shop.

When he was nineteen he met Sue. They were married at twenty one, the same year he bought his shop in East Ham, East London.

When I met Roy in 1972 he had had the shop for four years and Sue was pregnant. The baby was due in September.

Stevie joined Roy in 1970. Roy put him through an apprenticeship. This meant that Stevie had a day release to go to College in Hornchurch Essex every Monday to learn maths, English, biology and meat technology. It was a two year course and the exams were the equivalent to "A" levels. The rest of the week Stevie would learn his trade from Roy in the shop.

Being a busy precinct of shops, there were always deliveries being made. Roy's shop was in a precinct that had two butchers, two grocers, two greengrocers, a hardware shop, a pub, two newsagents, a florist a café, a launderette and more. You get the picture.

Roy, being Roy, knew that all delivery drivers had "overs". This meant that they had things on board that they shouldn't have. Basically, they had put them on the vehicle without anyone seeing and then they would sell them at a small cost to one of their regulars. So a delivery driver for a newsagent may have two boxes of jelly babies that are extra on board. He would then sell them to one of his drops at a discounted rate. The money went into his pocket and that was his beer money for the day. Everyone knew it went on and it was widely accepted. There was no CCTV in those days and it was impossible to check everything that went onto the vehicles.

As soon as Roy got the shop he started his onslaught of the delivery drivers. As soon as he saw any delivery being made to any shop in the precinct, he was off. He would run over to the driver and ask him directly, "Any overs mate?" Whether they said yes or no, he slipped them a few quid and said "Remember me next time, I'll take as much as you can get and I've always got cash."

This was music to most drivers' ears. They could normally get a lot of "overs" but the problem was getting rid of them. Not all shop keepers were like Roy. They may not always have the cash on them, they may not always want what the driver has. Now here was someone who was saying he would take anything and pay for it straightaway.

So within a few weeks it started, and true to his word Roy took anything and paid cash there and then. He was getting sweets, coffee, tea, sugar, towels - in fact, anything that was being delivered in our area, some of it was coming to Roy's shop. Roy had a large garage at the back of the shop and this was where everything was stored. Drivers now knew that they could load as many "overs" onto their vehicle as they wanted to and they could get rid of it easily.

Roy would then contact the other shops in the precinct and offer them goods at discounted prices; he would even give them an invoice. If he had a lot of one item, he would contact other shopkeepers in other areas and offer them the goods as well. He would make about a fifty percent mark up on everything and would earn some serious money. Everyone was happy.

It also worked the other way round. Shopkeepers would contact Roy and ask if he could get a certain item. Roy would speak to the relevant driver and say he would take as much as they could get of this particular item. He was now getting stuff to order.

So by the time I joined Roy in 1972, he was very well known in the area. He was known as the man who could get anything. The drivers simply knew Roy as "The Butcher".

And that brings you up to date and explains why Roy was so "popular".

But as with all these things, sometimes, no matter how savvy you are, you can get in too deep.

Chapter 6

Gambling and Kids

I'd been at the shop for about five months, working after school during the week and all day Saturday, and, as I mentioned earlier, I was also Roy's runner. It was always last minute with Roy: if the race was at 2.30, he would be looking at the paper at 2.28 and telling me to run as fast as I could at 2.29. I had to run across a busy road and into the bookies, write out the bet and then put it on. Sometimes I made it and sometimes I didn't. If I did and Roy was on, then all was okay. If the horse won and I was too late, Roy would blame me and I would blame Roy for being so "last minute." But it was all good banter.

Now back in 1972 if you had five pounds on a horse that was the equivalent of around forty pounds today. Roy's minimum bet was five pounds and maximum was fifty. Some day he would do very well, other days he would take a beating. Didn't make any difference to Roy, with everything that he had going on, money was no problem.

One Tuesday he had a fantastic day, he just couldn't stop winning. He had won around seven hundred pounds (more than three thousand pounds today). He was in no mood to stop when the day's horse racing finished. Stevie wasn't much of a gambler so he didn't show much interest, but I loved it. My Dad was a gambler and so was my Granddad, so I guess it was in my blood. Of course the good news was that if Roy won, he would always treat me. On this day he gave me fifty pounds. That was a lot of money for a kid of my age.

"Fancy coming to Romford dogs tonight?" he asked with that silly grin that he wore when he was up to mischief.

"Love to!" I replied.

So off we went to the dogs for the first race at 7.30pm. Roy picked me up in his new white sports car, an MGB GT. It was a bit of a girlie car but it could really move and Roy liked to drive like a maniac.

He was dropping me off again sixty minutes later. He had lost it all in three races and my fifty quid had gone as well. But he never moaned and still had a grin on his face when he drove off. When I saw him again the next day, it was mentioned once but never again. It just wasn't a big deal to Roy.

Soon it was July and the school six weeks holidays. Roy asked if I could work full time during those six weeks, which was great news. The shop closed at one o'clock on Mondays and Thursdays but all other week days were 07.00 until 18.00. He said he would pay me twenty five pounds. I jumped at the chance. My dad was earning the same money at the local gas works but he didn't get free meat.

So I worked full time in the shop during the school six week's holiday. Roy took Sue away on holiday for a couple of weeks to France. So it was just me and Stevie to run the shop. Two kids, one fourteen and one seventeen. It just couldn't happen today.

Of course we also had to look after the "extra" deliveries that came in. Roy left us with plenty of cash and said "Buy everything". So we did and just stored it in the garage until he came back.

All this time Roy was on the look-out for another shop. He kept it quiet, but at the beginning of September he told me and Stevie that he was taking over a shop in Plaistow, East London. It was a much bigger shop that had a big deli counter and also sold fresh bread, rolls and some groceries. It had four full time staff. The deal was completed at the end of September and a few days later Roy became a father. Sue had had twins! A boy and a girl. It was completely unexpected. It seems their heart beats were together and that's why it wasn't picked up before.

Roy was in shock. They had obviously only bought one of everything and now Roy had to go out and buy it all again. But typical Roy, he got it all done while Sue was in hospital and as an extra surprise for her he had the sign changed above the shop and the delivery van to "R.Marshall and Son".

The kids were christened Thomas and Sarah.

Roy took over the new shop on 1st October 1972; he kept all the existing staff on but asked Stevie to spend a couple of days a week over there just to keep an eye on things as the person he could trust. The new shop was taking two thousand five hundred pounds per week, which was twice as much as the East ham shop. Butchers work on a gross margin of thirty three percent. So out of the two shops combined he was earning around twelve hundred pounds. Once you took wages and overheads out Roy would clear around six hundred per week, which was great money back then. He was also earning about the same again from the "overs" he was getting in. The great thing about the new shop was that it sold a lot of things that Roy was getting from the delivery drivers. No longer did Roy have to sell on to other shopkeepers, he could now sell it in his own shop and make even more money.

Even with the extra responsibility of the twins, Roy still loved his bets and kept on gambling.

I was probably the only one who knew how much he was gambling. Sue never knew, she just thought it was a few quid here and there. Stevie didn't know, as he never got involved in any of it. Roy bet around a hundred pounds per day over a six day week. Some weeks he'd come out on top, other weeks were not so good, so it was hard to estimate. But overall he must have been losing at least two hundred pounds per week.

It didn't matter to Roy of course, because now he had two shops both making him money and of course, the "overs".

And Christmas was coming. Christmas was the Holy Grail for butchers. There was serious money to be made at Christmas.

Roy got his Turkeys from a farm in Norfolk and had done so ever since he had bought the shop back in 1968. Every year Roy would travel up to Norfolk and order his supply direct from the farmer. This year would be no exception, except that of course he needed to double his normal order. But this year the ride up to Norfolk would turn out to be a big adventure. Well, it was a big adventure for me…

Chapter 7

Norfolk and the Chair

The turkeys were delivered from Norfolk a week before Christmas, but not by the farmer. They were always delivered by his son. The farmer didn't drive a car. He drove tractors and other farm vehicles but didn't have a full licence for the road. He also didn't trust his son with Roy's money.

So he asked Roy if he could come to the farm a few weeks before and pay for the turkeys. Roy had done business with him for the past few years and trusted the old bastard enough to say yes. Besides, Roy wasn't the sort of man that you pissed off, so there was a kind of mutual respect and trust.

He asked me if I wanted to come along for the ride. We would go on a Sunday and be gone for most of the day. I thought it would be a great adventure; this turned out to be just the case.

The drive to Norfolk was slow. We went in Roy's van and to be honest it wasn't the quickest thing on the road. It took us about four hours to get there.

The farmer was pleased to see Roy and gave us some lunch, which consisted of cheese, bread, onion, cold turkey (of course) and a bottle of beer each. I loved it. He showed us around the farm, and was very proud of his turkeys. Roy gave him his order and paid his money, we left just after midday.

After about an hour's drive on the way back, Roy looked across at me and said "Fancy another beer?"

Silly question really. What does every fourteen year old boy want? Yes, BEER!

He pulled into a large car park just off of one of the small B roads that we had been travelling along. The sign above the pub door said "Lamb and Cutlass".

It was very much a local pub, full of character, oldie worldy, lots of framed pictures on the wall, roaring fire going right in the middle of the one bar, low ceilings (Roy had to duck as he went in). Of course back then every pub you went into was full of smoke, and this was no exception. You could hardly see the bar from the door, it was thick with cigarette smoke. He ordered two pints of bitter; the landlord gave him a look and then pointed to me.

"He's not old enough!"

Roy leaned over to the landlord and said quietly. "Sorry mate, he's my son, he's seventeen, eighteen next week to be honest, I know he looks a bit younger than that but he's with me and he's only having the one."

The landlord heard what Roy had said, but his expression didn't change. He looked at us with utter contempt.

"Okay, but just the one. Don't want to lose my license serving beer to under age strangers."

He walked away and pulled us two pints. We both heard him say under his breath,

"Bloody Londoners."

I could see Roy trying to hold his temper. He looked like he was about to jump the bar and lay one on the landlord. But he kept his calm and smiled at the landlord when he came back with our pints. We sat at the bar, quietly supping our beer. Roy looked at me and then over to the roaring fire.

"Now that is a fucking chair!"

He was looking at a big leather chesterfield fireside chair. Black leather, brass tacks, it really was a thing of beauty".

"Yeah it's nice Roy, really lovely. Bit big though."

"Rubbish, that would look great in the flat, Sue would love it. It's fucking quality is that".

"Yeah, it's nice Roy."

I had no idea at this stage how Roy's mind worked, but I was about to find out.

Roy leaned over and whispered.

"I'm going to the gents, when I come back make out your having chest pains and fall to the floor."

"What?"

"Go down, like you're having a heart attack or something as soon as I come out the gents."

"You joking?"

"No, just do it, I'll make it worth your while"

Roy got up and walked over to the gents. I wasn't quite sure what to do. Was it a wind up or was he serious?

But always thinking of making a few bob I remembered the words "Make it worth your while".

I saw Roy come out of the gents, then with a theatrical style I suddenly put both hands to my heart, stood up and started to cry out, I then fell to the floor, clutching my chest. The landlord ran from behind the bar and knelt down beside me.

"You okay, what's the matter? Is it a fit?"

A few of the locals gathered round as well.

"What's the matter with the kid?" someone shouted.

Roy was now making his way through the crowd.

"Let me through, let me through, it's the smoke, he's got weak lungs."

Roy knelt down beside me and gave me a wink.

"Let's get him outside and get him some fresh air. It's too smokey in here, his lungs can't cope."

Roy and the landlord got me up and helped me out of the pub into the car park. They sat me on the wall outside. Roy went quickly back into the pub and came out carrying the big chesterfield armchair.

"Here son, sit on this, take your time, get your breath back. That okay guvnor?"

The landlord's expression had changed. He now looked very apologetic.

"Of course, make him comfortable. Does he need a doctor or something?"

"No, just a bit of fresh air for a few minutes and he'll be fine. He was born with a dodgy left lung, so he gasps for air sometimes, especially when it's a smokey atmosphere and not enough ventilation."

The landlord looked mortified.

"I'm sorry son. We get used to it, but I can understand you being affected by it. Let me get you both a couple of pints."

The landlord went back in the pub along with the locals. Now it was only me and Roy outside, and of course the chair.

I looked at Roy, I couldn't believe what he had just done, it was sheer brilliance.

"You crafty bastard."

Roy laughed and then went quiet again as the landlord returned with two pints of bitter.

"These are on the house. Take your time, get your breath back."

"Thank you," I whispered in shallow breath.

We downed the pints quickly. Roy walked over to the other side of the car park and slowly drove the van and parked it next to me. Just as he did so the landlord walked back out of the pub. Roy got out of the van and very calmly spoke to the landlord.

"Thought I'd get the van as close to him as possible. He's still a bit weak, not sure his legs would carry him all the way across the car park. They say a brandy is good for shock, any chance?"

"Err, of course, let me get you two brandies."

Roy had done it again; he really did have more front than Brighton!

Two minutes later we were sipping large brandies outside the pub.

Then, very slowly and with no sense of urgency, we both stood up, I opened the back doors of the van, Roy picked up the chair and carefully placed it in the van. We both got in the front and Roy drove off.

We drove another hour before any of us spoke. I started laughing and then Roy started as well.

"Nice chair Roy, Sue's gonna love it."

"Yep and two nice brandy glasses as well."

The bastard had also nicked the two large brandy glasses. He started laughing.

"Bloody Londoners? That'll teach him to mess with bloody Londoners."

We got back to the shop later that day. Roy gave me twenty quid. I walked home feeling like I'd just stolen the crown jewels and got away with it.

The next morning I was at the shop at 07.00am. Roy was already working on the window display.

"Did she like the chair?" I inquired.

"Fucking hates it, says it's too big for the room, says I've got to get rid of it. Her dad's coming round later to take it back to their house."

I burst out laughing. We both laughed about it for the rest of the day.

Chapter 8

Christmas 1972

Christmas was just around the corner and now we really did have to work hard. This is a magic time of year for butchers. They can earn a fortune. It's very long hours, and very hard work, but also very good money.

I didn't go to school for the whole of December, and instead spent every day in the shop. I told Mum and Dad that there was nothing to do because of "exams", but told the school that a close relation had died and I was too upset to attend.

The week before Christmas we would work up to eighteen hours a day. I was shown how to "draw" a turkey, which means putting your hand inside the bird and "drawing" out its innards! Roy and Stevie would be cutting up and rolling beef or legs of pork (not much lamb was sold at Christmas), there were hams to boil, sausages to make, and fat to render down for dripping. I had learnt all these skills in the past six months.

Customers would start ordering their Christmas meat at the beginning of December; Roy also ran a Christmas club all year round and by the time Christmas came along there was a nice few quid in the club kitty. Before I started working in the butcher's shop I had no idea what a Christmas club was let alone knew how it worked. Once I realised what was going on I was shocked. I couldn't believe that it could even be legal. But it had been going on for years and just about every shop had one. On the face of it, it seems like a good idea. You start paying an amount of money each week to the butcher or baker or grocer and by Christmas you have enough money in your kitty to pay for all of your Christmas food. The reality is much different.

The great thing about a Christmas club is that people are paying for something in advance of getting it. Some people would even start their contributions in January, and many would have no idea how much they had put in, they would just put in a different amount every week (as much as they could afford). They would ask Roy in about October how much was in their club money. Roy, as bright as a button, would ask them how much they "thought" they had in there. If the customer said they had no idea or a rough figure, Roy would go away and calculate it a few pounds short of what it really was, and no one ever questioned it. Very few people actually kept their own record.

 Also, a lot of old people love a Christmas club, because it helps them budget their money and helps with the cost of Christmas. In fact I would say that as much as seventy five percent of the club money was put in by old ladies over sixty five. But of course by the time that Christmas came along, unfortunately some of these old ladies were no longer with us, so the money was just left in the kitty. Whatever way you looked at it, the Christmas club was a real money earner for Roy, and every other shopkeeper.

The orders came in thick and fast during December, so we knew what stock we had to get and also what we should get to sell at the last minute on Christmas Eve. That Christmas we sold over two hundred fresh turkeys - I know because I took the insides out of most of them!

Christmas Eve was manic, pure mayhem but great fun. We had bottles of sherry and whisky for the customers, and everyone who came in had a choice of drink. Some of the old girls got rather tipsy and I can still hear one old lady, well in her seventies, singing "Long Haired Lover from Liverpool" by Jimmy Osmond at the top of her voice whilst doing the can – can.

On Christmas Eve, I left the shop at 16.00, the most tired I had ever been in all of my fourteen years. I had started at 04.30 that morning and the night before that we had finished at 22.00.

My wages for the week was one hundred pounds. Roy and Stevie also gave me all the money that was in the "tip" box. This was a box that we put on the counter at the beginning of December and customers would put in their "tips". The tip box gave me an extra forty five pounds.

It was the most money I had ever had; the problem was that having been at work all the time I hadn't bought any Christmas presents. So on the way home I bought a Christmas card for Mum, Dad and Ruth and put twenty pounds in each.

I got home and once again fell asleep; Mum didn't have the heart to wake me so I slept on the settee all night until 09.00 the next morning. Exhaustion had kicked in and for the next two days I was physically ill. Sick, shivers, the lot.

I missed Christmas in 1972.

One thing that I didn't notice but everyone else did, was that I was getting bigger, much bigger. Since I started in March, I had put on two stone, all muscle. I was no longer a skinny kid; I was strong without an ounce of fat. Hard manual work and eating lots of steaks had really kicked in.

I began to notice things around me differently as well, and when I went back to school after the Christmas break, I missed Roy and Stevie. I was now back amongst kids again but I was used to being with men. I was used to adult humour and conversations, swearing, satire and women. There were always lots of yummy mummies coming in who you could have a laugh and joke with. Being with kids my own age no longer seemed fun.

Chapter 9

A Career Decision

1973 was all about work. Not school work of course, shop work.

I practically gave up on school that year, just started turning up at the shop, even when I wasn't asked to, I just sort of popped in, put on a white coat and started working. Mum and Dad were told that this year was all about exams and study time, so they never questioned it. The school couldn't care less as I would be leaving in twelve months anyway.

Roy would ask me at the end of the week, what days I had worked and would pay me accordingly. He would always give me a bit of a bonus as well, normally a couple of quid and then get me a joint of meat from the fridge. The family had never eaten so much meat in all their lives.

The extra weight and muscle I had put on made me look a bit older than my fifteen years. I had also grown in height by a couple of inches, and people that hadn't seen me for a while like, aunts and uncles, couldn't believe how much I'd changed. I suddenly looked like an eighteen year old. I had always been lucky with looks but now, what with the muscular physique, I was having to fight off the girls as well. Roy and Stevie were always taking the piss; they noticed that on Saturdays young girls were coming in with their Mums just to see the " Butcher Boy". Lots of smiles and giggles were going on.

I lost my virginity that year to a beautiful blonde haired sixteen year old girl called Deborah. She came in with her mum one Saturday and kept giving me the eye. As she left, I ran after her and asked her if she wanted to go out sometime. She said yes and we agreed to go out that same night. I knocked on her door at seven thirty as arranged, her mum opened the door and said she was upstairs in her bedroom and that I could go up. As soon as I closed the door she started taking all her clothes off and then mine, it was one of the best twenty minutes of my life. I went out with a lot of girls in 1973.

Back at the shop, I was now serving customers, taking the money, learning how to cut up pigs, hind and fore quarters of beef, even how to bone out intricate things like pig heads.

And still of course the most important job…making tea.

Stevie was spending most of his time at the Plaistow shop. So apart from an old part-timer who came in a couple of afternoons a week, it was just me and Roy running things in East Ham.

Towards the end of 1973, Roy asked me what I wanted to do when I left school. There was of course only one answer. Butcher!

Roy got me on a butchery course at the College for the Distributive Trades in Briset Street, which was close to Smithfield Market and most people knew it as Smithfield College. It was the same course that Roy had done years earlier but mine was a day release course whereas his had been evening classes.

I was told that I could start in January 1974, every Monday between 08.30 and 16.30. The rest of the week I would learn my trade at the shop. It was a three year course but if you were good enough you may be able to finish it in two. I decided straight away that I was going to be the best butcher they'd ever seen.

Mum and Dad weren't happy about it, but were very supportive because they knew this was the only thing that I wanted to do. Like all parents they'd hoped that their son would become a doctor or a lawyer or at the very least a mechanic at Fords. No chance, I wanted to be a Master butcher.

I wanted to be just like Roy and have a chain of butcher's shops all over the East End.

Roy also decided that as part of my "education", I should accompany him to Smithfield market once a week and see how things worked down there. He picked me up on the first visit at 04.30am. Now Smithfield Market is a scary place even for grown men, let alone a fifteen year old boy. But I was with Roy and I knew I'd be okay.

Smithfield at 5.00am is the busiest place on the planet. It feels like utter chaos is going on everywhere. If you're not careful you could get crushed by the crowd. The first thing I noticed was the smell. I thought the butchers shop smelt fantastic, imagine that smell multiplied by a thousand.

Then there are the sounds. There's shouting from every direction. "Mind your backs", is all you hear as the porters take peoples meat to their vehicles, but some weren't so polite. "Get the fuck out the way you wankers!" Roy would simply shout back "Look where you're going you cunt."

A number of times I thought there was going to be a fight, but realised this was just the way things were down here. Roy took me over to his old wholesaler shop where he had worked and gave one of his old mates a wink.

"Hello you gib deelow teenuc. How about evif beemals?" Everyone seemed to talk in backslang, Roy had just called this bloke a big old cunt and ordered five lambs, but it was all friendly and good banter.

"Roy, good to see you mate, still got the pox all over your cock?"

"Yeah, must have caught it from fucking your wife."

Everyone laughed and then Roy's mate put five lambs on the scale.

The weight was agreed at 176lbs and Roy was given a ticket. A porter came up and took the lambs away. Roy went to the cashier and paid cash. He then shouted out loud.

"Okay you lot, I'm fucking off now, can't stand around all day talking to a load of wankers like you."

A hurl of abuse came Roy's way, some old off cuts of lamb were thrown at us and we walked away being called every swear word you can imagine.

Roy turned and looked at me.

"I fucking love it down here."

I had to admit, so did I.

We got back to Roy's van and met the porter. His trolley had not five but seven lambs on it. Roy unlocked the back doors of the van and the meat was put inside. Roy shook the porter's hand and it was obvious that he had also slipped him a bundle of notes as well.

"Cheers Roy, see you next week."

Roy then introduced me.

"This is Joe. He's my new butcher. He starts at Smithfield College in January, if he ever comes down here without me, look after him okay?"

"No problem Roy, good as done." He then turned to me and gave me a smile.

"Nice to meet you Joe, if you want a beer when you start college, we all drink in the Three Compasses. We're in there every day from about ten till midday, anytime just come in and we'll look after you."

"Cheers mate."

We shook hands, the porter left, and me and Roy got in the van and headed back to the shop.

We were passing through Stepney when Roy spotted something. He stopped the van.

"We could be in luck here Joe."

I had no idea what he was talking about. It was only half past five in the morning and the streets were deserted.

"What?"

Roy smiled.

"Up the street about 100 yards. See that lorry that's just pulled up outside the chicken shop?"

I looked and sure enough there was a large lorry stopping outside a KFC.

"And what's that got to do with us?"

Roy was watching intently.

"In a minute the driver will get out and start unloading boxes of chicken. He'll place them outside the shop in the doorway. He's early because in an hour's time the traffic round here will be a nightmare and he wants to get on with the rest of his round. The shop manager will probably get here around seven. So for the next hour or so there will be cases of chicken just left outside. Now you see?"

I did. We were going to nick them.

It happened exactly as Roy had said. The driver got out, unloaded six cases of chicken, got back in his lorry and drove off.

We waited for five minutes then casually drove up to the shop loaded the cases of chicken on the van and off we went. I couldn't believe how easy it was.

We were back at the shop and unloaded by 6.00am. It was, as Roy had put it, "An Education."

I left school early (you could in those days), just before Christmas 1973. Once again Christmas was manic and even busier than the year before. But this year I survived without being seriously ill!

On the 28th January 1974 I was sixteen. Dad bought me a ticket to see Muhammad Ali against Joe Frazier. In those days you had to go to certain cinemas to see it live. It started at 04.00am, but to see the undercard you had to get there around midnight. I loved these occasions and went to see all of Ali's fights.

Roy bought me my own set of steak and boning knives. I was thrilled.

So in January 1974, I officially left school to pursue a career as a trainee shopman / cutter (butcher) at R.Marshall and Sons, High Road, East Ham, London E6.

Chapter 10

Gary and the Greyhound Misunderstanding

Stevie told me that Roy had a bit of a temper but I'd never seen it. To me his bark was always bigger than his bite. Don't get me wrong, Roy was a hard man, he had to be coming from where he came from, but up until then I'd never seen him lose his temper. But I was to see it twice in just a few weeks. The first time was with a local gang member.

Now there were a few gangs in our area. Mainly eighteen to twenty year olds finding their way in the world, sorting out their pecking order. The "leader" of one gang was a guy called Gary. He was early twenties, good looking with black hair and always dressed in expensive clothes. He drove a big flash American car. He and his group of mates drank in the pub opposite the shop.

Gary really thought he was the business. He came into the shop one Thursday afternoon just as we were about to close. He told Roy he could get "a load of meat". Pigs, lambs, chickens, he couldn't be specific about the quantity but it would be a van full and it would all be fresh. If Roy was interested he could deliver it to the shop early the next morning.

Roy agreed. It was perfect timing. Friday and Saturday's were the busiest days of the week and he could do with as much meat as he could get. Especially if it was cheap, he could do some special offers. He told Gary he would take the lot. Gary said he would be at the shop at 4.30am the next morning.

When I arrived at the shop just before seven o'clock Roy was smiling. He and Stevie were in mid conversation about the delivery. Gary had arrived just as he said he would and the large walk in fridge was crammed full of fresh meat. Three pigs, six lambs, various cases of different size chickens and various tubs of offal.

We started to do the window display. At seven o'clock the phone rang. Roy answered it. I couldn't hear the conversation, but I watched him. He listened carefully and every now and again said a few words. He put the phone down and looked at Stevie and me.

"I'm gonna kill that cunt."

Stevie looked confused.

"What's happened, what's wrong, who was on the phone."

"It was old Fred."

Old Fred owned a small lock up butcher's shop about a mile away.

There were three Butchers shop in our local area. There was Roy's, Palmers, which was another family butchers just across the road from our shop and then there was Old Fred's, about a mile away. Although the shops were in competition with each other, they all helped each other out from time to time. There was a mutual respect for one another. So if Roy ran out of drumsticks or something, we would phone the other two and borrow a box then replace it next time he went down the market. Same for Fred, he would often phone up and say he'd just had a big order come in and could he "borrow" a couple of Lambs for a few days. In this area everyone helped each other.

Old Fred was in his late sixties, he'd arrived at his shop that morning only to find he'd been burgled and cleaned out. He'd called Roy to see if he had any meat he could spare for the weekend. He was desperate. Without meat he couldn't open the shop and would have to let his regulars down.

Me and Stevie loaded up Roy's van with as much as we could and Roy drove it round to Old Fred's. Roy never told Fred about Gary, he was too embarrassed. He told Fred that the meat was a freebie and he was sure that Fred would do the same for him if he was in the same predicament.

When he got back he was still fuming.

"Did no one ever teach that little slag not to shit on his own doorstep?"

I'd known Roy for a while now but he had a look on his face that I hadn't seen before. It was a look that said "Trouble." All morning he was quiet, he served the customers as usual but he just wasn't himself. He kept looking at the clock. I wondered why.

At half past twelve he finished serving a customer, put down his tools and looked at me and Stevie.

"Right, the pubs open. Time to teach that cunt a lesson."

He walked out of the shop, across the road and into the pub. The shop was still quite busy and Stevie was busy serving customers and I was re-stocking the window display. Then one of the customers, a nice old lady who was at the back of the queue, put down her bag and spoke to Stevie.

"What's Roy up to?"

She, along with the other customers was staring across the road. I looked over.

Roy had Gary up against the pub wall. I didn't see the punch, but suddenly saw Gary double up in pain and fall to the floor. Roy dragged him to his feet and hit him again. Gary's hands were above his head in an act of surrender. I saw him empty his pockets and give Roy something. Roy wagged his finger at him and then walked back towards the shop. For some strange reason we all went back to what we were doing and pretended we hadn't seen a thing. Roy walked back into the shop and joined Stevie behind the counter. He smiled at one of the woman.

"What can I get you darling?"

He just carried on as though nothing had happened.

We never heard from Gary or any of his mates again. For some reason they decided to drink in another pub.

The second time was just a few weeks later. With all this money coming in, Roy decided he would buy a greyhound and run it at Romford. Although he loved a bet, he had no idea about buying a greyhound or getting it trained. But his old mate Mark who he used to work with down at the market already owned three and raced them at Walthamstow.

He called Mark and they decided to buy one between them. Mark said he would arrange it all and would ask his trainer at Walthamstow if there were any pups for sale.

Within a month Mark and Roy were the proud owners of a two year old brindle bitch called Mellow Maisy. It had come over from Ireland and had trialled well on one of the Irish tracks. It was a short to middle distance dog and would be ideal for Romford.

They decided to put it with a trainer called Ronny Gray. He was known as a bit of a wide boy who liked a gamble. He often had dogs running at ten to one that everyone thought were no hopers but would mysteriously win.

After three or four trial runs around Romford's tight track, Ronny decided it was time the dog should run a proper race. It wasn't the fastest dog in the world but was far from being the slowest. It was graded as a grade three dog. Grade one being the best and grade eight the lowest.

Ronny told Mark and Roy that it had an excellent chance of winning its first race, and the price would be good as it was an unknown quantity - this was its first proper race.

We all went to Romford to see Mellow Maisy on its debut.

The whole of the Marshall clan were there, all the brothers and their wives, aunts, uncles, mums and dads (mine included). There must have been around thirty of us.

Maisy was in the fourth race of the night. She was a six to one shot. Roy had a thousand pounds to win and so did Mark. I had one hundred.

The traps opened and out came Maisy, stone last. She finished the race twelve lengths behind the winner.

There was a kind of stunned hush over all of us. We couldn't believe what we had just seen.

Roy and Mark went to see Ronny Gray. Mark was the first to ask the questions.

"What the fuck happened? You said it had a fair chance, it was rubbish!"

Ronny was not intimidated by Mark, which was a big mistake because Mark had a fearsome temper and was a well-known boxer in the East End.

"Listen, these things happen, it must have hurt itself in the traps. Dogs can do that sometimes, bruise their paw and then don't want to run. I'll have it checked over by the vet and let you know."

Ronny Gray walked off. No apology, no remorse, nothing.

Mark wanted to kill him, but Roy calmed him down.

"Look, as he said, she's probably hurt herself in the traps. It's just one of those things."

They came back and bought a round of drinks for everyone. But I could see by their faces they weren't going to let it go.

Two weeks later and Maisy was going to run again. This time there was only going to be three of us to see it run; everyone else was convinced it was a rubbish dog. So just me, Roy and Mark made our way to Romford Dogs in Mark's new Bentley.

Mark had done really well since leaving the Market. Like Roy, he had saved a small fortune from his ill-gotten gains and had invested wisely. He bought an old warehouse in East London and converted it into an abattoir. He was now supplying his old shop down the market and a number of others as well.

Maisy opened up at ten to one; no one gave her a chance. We saw Ronny Gray and he said the same as last time.

"It's got a real chance tonight boys, a really good chance."

Roy and Mark both had a thousand pounds each on it and I had my usual one hundred.

The traps opened and out came Maisy, stone last yet again; once again she finished well behind the five other dogs.

Mark was ready to rip the trainers head off but Roy talked him out of it.

"Let's have a drink and decide what we're going to do."

We did. In fact we had four of five drinks. We watched the winning owner collect his trophy and shake hands with the sponsor. Then about ten minutes later Roy spotted something.

"Hey Mark, look over there right at the end of the bar, it's our trainer Ronny Gray having a beer with the owner of the winning dog."

Sure enough, there was Ronny drinking what looked like a large scotch with the owner of the winning dog, all smiles and laughs. Then the owner slipped him something very casually along the bar. Ronny picked it up and put it in his inside pocket, they shook hands and Ronny headed for the toilet.

Mark stood up.

"Cunt!"

This time Roy never tried to calm him down. His face had gone bright red and he had that look that I'd seen a few weeks ago just before he went over to the pub and beat up Gary. They both marched off to the toilets. I followed.

I was told to stay outside and not let anyone in.

"Say it's being cleaned, someone's been ill."

The other two went into the toilets; three old guys came out looking scared. Obviously Roy and Mark had told them to fuck off so as to leave just them and Ronny Gray alone.

To this day I don't know exactly what happened during those ten minutes in the toilets but Ronny Gray appeared first, his head and shoulders soaking wet and a dribble of blood from his mouth. He looked absolutely terrified and was trying to catch his breath. Two minutes later Roy and Mark appeared as though nothing had happened. We all got into Mark's Bentley and drove back.

Mellow Maisy won four races in a row after that night, and Mark and Roy won close to twenty grand each before they "retired" her six months later.

Whenever we went to Romford dogs and we bumped into Mr Gray, he always sent a drink over for us. Must have just been a misunderstanding!

Chapter 11

Sparman, Bernie and Tiny Tim

About a mile and a half away was a local Spar. The manager was a bit posh for our area and Roy never really got on with him. He spoke with a bit of a plumb in his mouth, and we were sure he'd gone to public school. But he definitely had an eye for business. He came to see Roy one day and asked if he would supply his Spar shop with some meat. A deal was struck. Roy would supply meat in polystyrene trays covered with cling film and put price stickers on them. The price would be ten percent more than we charged in the shop. Roy would charge Spar ten percent less than we charged, so Spar would make twenty percent profit on everything they sold. Everyone was happy.

Spar weren't interested in making a huge profit; they just wanted to provide an extra product that they didn't already have. It worked well and after a few weeks Spar would order every morning at seven thirty by telephone. It was my job to put the order together and then Stevie would make the delivery at eight thirty in Roy's van.

Roy thought this was the way forward and decided to offer the same kind of deal to other grocer shops outside of the area. He approached a small grocers shop in Limehouse. The shop was owned by a mountain of a man called Bernie. Bernie owned another shop in Stepney.

We provided the same service for both of Bernie's shops. It was the same routine as for Spar, Bernie would phone over his order sometime between seven and seven thirty, I would get the orders together and then Stevie would deliver to Bernie's shops after dropping off the Spar order.

Although Bernie was well over six foot, around twenty stone and looked like he could kill you with his bare hands, he was in fact a gentle giant. He spoke softly, had a tremendous laugh and a great sense of humour. He and Roy became mates very quickly.

Roy supplied Bernie with a lot of groceries for his two shops. Whatever "overs" came into the shop, Roy would always think of Bernie first and most of the time Bernie said yes and Stevie would drop the goods off at the same time as Bernie's meat order. Bernie always seemed to have loads of cash and paid for everything straightaway.

Bernie approached Roy one day about some wine. He said that in his Stepney shop he had a small off licence section. His best seller was sherry. He ordered his sherry from a wholesaler in Shoreditch. Bernie sold around ten cases of Sherry a week. His regular delivery driver was an extremely short man called Tim. He was always asking Bernie if he wanted any wine. It seemed that the wine section of the warehouse was virtually free of any security. The reason being that hardly anyone drank wine back in the seventies. In fact if you went to a restaurant your choices would have been "Blue Nun" or "Mateus Rose" and that was about it. Drinking wine just wasn't a working class thing to do and you didn't get more working class then the East End of London.

Tim was keen to find someone who would buy it in quantity. He knew he could get lots of it but had no wanted to take it.

Bernie declined Tim's kind offer, knowing that no one in his area would buy it. But knowing what Roy was like, gave Tim Roy's name and address. Bernie called Roy and told him about the wine. Roy thanked Bernie and waited.

He didn't have to wait long. Two days later a large transit pulled up outside the shop. A small man got out who looked as though he ought to be a jockey. He walked into the shop and waited until I had finished serving a customer.

"Is Roy the Butcher about mate?"

Unfortunately Roy was out.

"Sorry mate he's just popped out. I can help though. Is it about the wine?"

The driver seemed surprised that this sixteen year old boy was in charge.

"Yes mate, Bernie said you might want some."

"Yep, how much you got?"

"Just six cases today but I can get more, a lot more."

"Lovely, we'll take the six and whatever you can get in future."

Tiny Tim unloaded six cases of wine and I paid him thirty quid, five pound a case. There were twelve bottles in each case. I didn't have a clue if that was cheap or not, or whether it was white or red or sweet or dry, I just did a Roy and bought it. Tiny Tim was thrilled.

"Cheers mate. I pass here twice a week. You sure you want it that often?"

"Yes mate, as much and as often as you can."

He jumped back in his van a happy man.

Roy returned to the shop about two hours later. I showed him the wine.

"Nice one, seventy two bottles for thirty quid seems cheap to me. We'll put a few bottles in the window tomorrow when we do the display let's see if any of the customers want it at a seventy five pence a bottle."

And that's what we did. We put six red and six white in the window the next morning. All Roy knew was that red wine went with red meat so six bottles went in with the trays of steaks and the six white went amongst the trays of chicken and pork.

As the customers began to come in on that Friday morning, we would ask them if they fancied a bottle of wine to go with their meat. Only seventy five pence. We sold out before midday.

The following Tuesday a 7.5t lorry pulled up outside the shop. Out jumped Tiny Tim. This time Roy was in the shop.

The driver ignored Roy and came over to me where I was cutting up some lambs.

"Hello mate, got a bit more wine for you if you want it."

Roy looked over. Part of him was amused but I think he was also a bit miffed that the driver thought I was the main man.

"Excuse me mate, it's me you want, the boy's only in charge when I'm not here."

"Sorry guvnor. Got some more wine for you."

Roy walked out of the shop with the tiny man. I couldn't help thinking how funny the two of them looked. Roy who was well over six foot and the driver who was under five!

I saw them shake hands and Roy came back into the shop laughing.

"Joe, you better go out there and give him a hand. He's only got thirty five fucking cases for us."

Sure enough he had. This time Roy did a deal with him, he said he would take whatever he could get no matter what volume but the price would have to be four pound a case. The driver agreed, happy that he had found someone who would take the quantity. As I said before, wine wasn't a big thing back then.

Roy wasted no time in getting it placed. There was a big and quite famous Steak House a few miles away and we supplied them with steaks and sausages twice a week. Roy took a few cases to them to have a look at; they jumped at it for eighty pence per bottle. From then on they had thirty cases a week from Roy. We sold between five and ten cases a week in the shop, but that still left us with some more to shift. Some weeks Tiny Tim could bring us one hundred cases. Roy always took it and paid cash there and then, Bernie took a couple every week and then Roy approached the manager of the local Spar. He turned out to be a real wine buff and belonged to a wine tasting club. He also took twenty cases a week. Ten of these he sold in his shop and the others he sold to his wine buff friends.

Roy now had a way of getting rid of around sixty or seventy cases a week and doubling his money. The great thing about the wine was that it didn't go off, if anything it got better. Roy had already earned his money on the cases he sold so if at the end of the week he had ten cases over we just stuck them in Roy's garage or his brother's lock up. There was always a customer with a large family party or a wedding coming up and everyone knew that Roy had wine, so he would sell them half a dozen cases.

In the mid to late seventies, wine bars started opening all over East London. People seemed to have acquired a taste for it. I wonder, if in some small way, Roy had played a part in that?

Chapter 12

A Record Business

So far, apart from the regular wine delivery, it was only a few cases of this and that and Roy could cope with it easily, but in 1974 things were about to get a whole lot bigger and Roy was to move up a gear.

Sometime in August one of our regular customers, an attractive lady called Tina, mid- thirties, brown hair and amazing cleavage, asked Roy is she could have a quiet word. She said her husband had some records and tapes for sale and would Roy be interested in buying them. Music to Roy's ears, excuse the pun. He of course said yes. Tina said her husband would call in the shop the next day.

Sure enough early the next day a tall thin guy called Trevor came into the shop and asked for Roy. I called out for him and the three of us went out to the back of the shop while Stevie served. Now although Stevie was older than me and had been with Roy longer, Roy liked me in on these things. I think he realised that I was just like him, I loved the thrill of a scam whereas Stevie really couldn't be bothered.

This was the deal.

Trevor had a job as a night security guard for a large wholesale and mail order record company in Essex. They were huge and were the largest mail order music company in the UK. If you opened a magazine or Sunday supplement in those days, this company would have a full colour page of advertising. "Join our music club today and we'll send you two free records or tapes for free and every month we'll send you the No 1 record or tape at a discounted price." They practically invented junk mail in this country, and were a household name at that time.

Trevor said that the security was non- existent at night and he had soon realised that he could wander around the warehouse and help himself to records and tapes then load them into his car. He was the only one on at night and he was in charge. There was no CCTV back then of course, it was just one security guard and that was him. He said the warehouse was massive and it was floor to ceiling with records and tapes. There didn't seem to be any stock control and no check on him or his car. He'd been there for three months and realised that he could take what he wanted. He and his family had enough and thought he would now branch out and make a few quid.

Roy's face beamed. "Great, get everything you can and I'll have the lot." Now at this stage Roy had no idea how he was going to get rid of it and also no idea how much stuff would be coming in, but true to form he never said no.

Trevor's night shift started at 18.00 and finished at 06.00, and so we agreed that he would come to the shop on his way home at around 06.30 and drop off anything that he'd got during the night.

I'll never forget the first day he came over. I got to the shop early to have a look. At about 06.45 Trevor arrived but not in a car, in a small van. He pulled up outside the shop and called me over to help. As he opened the doors of the van, I stood back and laughed. It was full from floor to ceiling with LPs, singles and tapes. Hundreds and hundreds of them. All three of us unloaded the van as quickly as possible and put them at the back of the shop. Roy said he would pay Trevor the next day as soon as he worked out exactly what he had. Trevor said "No problem", and off he went.

"Same again tomorrow. I can get this amount everyday if you want?"

"Keep it coming," was all Roy could say.

Roy didn't know whether to laugh or cry, this was far bigger than we had ever imagined. LPs and cassette tapes were selling for around two pounds in 1974 and on that first day we had three hundred and fifty of them. So the retail value was seven hundred pound in one day. If he could get this amount five days a week, that would be three thousand five hundred pounds worth. That's about twenty thousand pounds by today's value. Or, one million per year. This was big, very big.

Roy agreed to pay Trevor forty pence for each one. Trevor was delighted with this, it meant that he was getting well over one hundred pounds per day, a real nice sum of money back in 1974. Roy worked out that he could probably get one pound each so would earn a nice few quid. But of course he had to find someone to buy the bloody things first.

There were three major record shops in the area, but Roy was reluctant to try to sell to any of them. Too many questions would be asked. But, there was a small newsagents about half a mile up the road, called Meads. Roy had sold them some odds and sods over the years. They also had a small sideline in selling records. Mainly the top ten singles and albums. Roy knew Paul, the guy who owned it, quite well and they went for a beer. Roy came clean and told him what he was getting, but obviously not where from. They agreed a deal at eighty pence each provided that Meads took everything. Paul said that he'd always been keen to expand that part of his business but his wife was happy just selling sweets and newspapers. This seemed like the opportunity he'd been waiting for.

It worked a treat. Trevor would drop off whatever he had every morning. I would sort them out (obviously taking out any soul / funk albums that took my eye) and Roy would take the rest of them to Meads every afternoon. Meads were now able to undercut the opposition in the area by thirty three percent. They were selling albums at one pound forty nine and everywhere else they were one ninety nine.

At the end of 1974, Meads Newsagents became Meads Records and Tapes; they opened four other shops in Essex in 1975.

Roy was now earning serious money. This little deal was giving him between six hundred and one thousand pounds per week depending on what was coming in. On top of that he was earning another four hundred pounds from the other bits and pieces and then he had his "proper" earnings from the two shops.

And if Roy was earning good money, so was I. For helping with the records I was given another fifty pounds every week. I was now clearing more than one hundred and fifty quid per week, which was four times as much as my dad and I was only sixteen.

Roy had moved up a gear, and he was now in a different league. Word was getting round that here was a guy that could get and get rid of, practically anything. This was serious stuff. However, it would soon become far more serious.

Chapter 13

Gaz and The Corned Beef

The next year we started to get a few "faces" calling into the shop. By this I mean local villains. Word had got round that Roy was a player and somebody to be associated with.

One such "face" was Gaz. Gaz lived in Dagenham and suffered from curvature of the spine. Because of this he walked with a kind of shuffle, all hunched up. He had the strangest of hair. It wasn't ginger, it wasn't brown, but a sort of orangey colour. It was very thin and wispy; he always looked like he'd just walked in from out of a storm. He spoke in a very low guttural voice like he'd smoked two hundred cigarettes a day all his life. He ended every sentence with the words "you know what I mean?" He looked fifty but was only in his mid- thirties.

But Gaz, no matter how strange he was, was a local face. He had a similar reputation to Roy, he could get things. He didn't have a real job, didn't claim any benefits, lived in a small council house and drove an old beaten up Ford MK1 Cortina. He was under the radar, and that's just how Gaz liked it. No one paid him any attention.

Gaz liked Roy, and I am sure that Roy had a liking for Gaz. He became a regular in the shop. He would often be there when I turned up at 06.45. He and Roy would be having a cup of tea and talking about what gear they had or what was coming up. So far it was just talk and they hadn't actually done any deals together. That was soon to change and would catapult Roy into an even bigger league. We also saw a different side to Gaz early one morning.

A van driver came in and gave us the usual spiel.

"I've just laid some carpet for a massive company just up the road and have got a nice piece left over. Interested?"

Now of course we knew this was a load of bollocks. He had gone to a warehouse and bought an off cut of cheap carpet. It would have a small flaw in it or a hole in the middle. He would hope that he didn't have to roll it out and normally he didn't have to. He would make a small profit on it. But if he did that a few times every day he would earn himself a few quid. Roy and I saw these guys every few weeks and would just say "No thanks mate" and that would be the end of it.

But this day Gaz was with us. He looked at the guy selling the carpet and then picked up one of our boning knives. He walked up to the guy, who was twice his size, looked him in the eyes and said.

"What do you take us for, a bunch of cunts? Now take your carpet and fuck off before I cut your eyes out."

The guy fucked off. He was terrified, and, I have to say both Roy and I were also a bit nervous.

Gaz came in the shop one morning to see Roy. He asked him if he needed any corned beef. Roy of course just laughed and told Gaz he would take as much as he could get. Gaz explained that in the next couple of days he would have a "load" of corned beef, around a thousand tins. Once again Roy said no problem, he would have the lot; he could shift it easily with all the grocer contacts he had. No big deal. The price was agreed. Roy told Gaz he would buy it for a quarter of the price that it sold for in the shops.

Two days later Roy got the call from Gaz. The corned beef was on its way. Roy told Gaz to bring it round to the service road at the back of the shop. About an hour later Gaz walked into the shop with a huge grin on his face

"It's here Roy, but not quite what we were expecting."

Roy was intrigued, and the three of us walked round to the service road at the back of the shop. There in front of us, blocking the whole of the road was a 40ft container on the back of a huge rig.

"What the fuck." said Roy. "Don't tell me that's full of fucking corned beef?"

"Absolutely jammed packed," laughed Gaz.

I walked forward to open the door with Gaz laughing behind me.

"Be careful son!" he said "Don't want you to get trampled!" I of course though he was talking about the corned beef but was about to get the shock of my life

As I opened the doors of the container, I could hear a noise. It sounded like muffled speech. Then something large fell out onto the road and made me jump out of my skin. It was a man's body. A cloth bag over his head and hands tied behind his back. He was lying in the middle of the road and kept saying "Please don't kill me, please don't kill me."

Gaz thought this was hilarious, but Roy and I were in shock. Only then did it start to sink in. Gaz and his mate had hi-jacked this lorry and bundled the driver into the back. Roy and I led the man into the garage, told him to be quiet and everything would be ok. The poor guy actually wet himself. We both felt sorry for him, but had to act as though we were used to this sort of thing.

"Okay, we need to shift this lot asap," said Gaz. "Joe get on the back and start unloading, everyone else start getting this lot into the garage."

It was only then that we realised what we had. This wasn't one thousand little tins of corned beef. This was two hundred and fifty cases of catering tins of corned beef. Each case had six, six pound tins in it. That's over eight tonnes of the stuff. How the fuck was Roy going to get rid of this lot?

We started to unload, which took about an hour. There were cases of corned beef everywhere, and not only was it heavy, it was bulky as well. Each case weighed over 35lb or 17 kilos. The garage was full, the cutting room at the back of the shop was full, and we couldn't get any more in the walk in fridge. Everywhere you went there was fucking corned beef.

I took a van load round to my Mum and Dad's house and put twenty cases in Dad's shed. Roy's brother took another twenty five cases and stored these in his lock up in Poplar. The Plaistow shop took about another thirty. By the end of the day we had managed to get it all out of the way.

Gaz and his mates took the lorry away, with the driver loaded in the back, still tied up. He said he would take it to a trailer park about thirty miles away and then call the old bill a few hours later so they could find the poor old sod and let him out. As he drove off Gaz shouted to Roy that he would be back in a few days to get his money.

Now the hard work would begin. Who the fuck would want fifteen hundred giant tins of corned beef?

The great thing about Roy was that he had front. He had more front than fucking Brighton.

The next day, he decided to go along to a cash and carry that he used from time to time in Bow. He wanted to see what the price was for these catering tins of corned beef. He couldn't start selling them until he knew what they were worth. He also had to agree a price with Gaz, but he couldn't do this either unless he knew what they were being sold for.

While he was there he thought he'd take a chance and ask the owner if he wanted any corned beef. This was a bit risky as the hi-jack was being reported in a couple of the national newspapers along with a quote from the poor driver who said he been threatened with his life. Not quite true.

He asked one of the girls on the tills if he could speak with the guvnor. She pointed to an Indian man called Mr. Patel. Roy came straight to the point. He simply said he had acquired a large quantity of corned beef and would Mr. Patel be interested in buying any?

Mr. Patel took Roy to his office and they agreed a deal there and then. Mr. Patel owned six cash and carries in the UK; he supplied most of the Asian supermarkets in East London, Birmingham, Bradford and Leeds. Like a lot of Asian business men, Mr. Patel liked to deal in cash.

When Roy came back to the shop later that day, his face was a picture. "We've had a right result today Joe, you'll earn yourself a nice few quid for helping out mate."

He told me the full story about his meeting with Mr Patel.

I remember saying to him, "You're the jammiest sod I've ever met. You've got more Jam than Hartleys."

Over the next few days, Roy and I moved the corned beef to one of Mr. Patel's warehouses. Roy hired a 7.5t lorry and it took us four trips and all day. Stevie looked after the shop along with the old part timer. As I said before, Stevie had no real taste for this kind of stuff, he just wanted to get on with the butchery work. Me? I couldn't get enough of it.

Gaz came by four days later. I think he was expecting Roy to ask for a bit more time to pay up. But Roy gave him a cup of tea and then paid him out in crisp new pound notes.

Gaz walked away a very happy man. Roy had made a nice few grand in just a few days and I was given a few hundred quid for my bit.

The corned beef job turned out to be a big turning point for Roy, it proved to a lot of people that he really could get, and shift, anything. Gaz was impressed and must have told a few of his contacts, because after that we started to get more and more characters coming into the shop with all sorts of deals.

Mr. Patel was also going to play a big part over the next eighteen months.

Chapter 14

Colin and The Cousins

After the corned beef job, we had a similar delivery every few weeks. The deal would be the same. Gaz would call Roy, say he was on his way and that we should be ready to unload.

Over the next six months we had a variety of goods. One load was cowboy boots. We had three thousand pairs of them. These were very popular in 1975; well, at least they were in East London. Roy decided that instead of trying to sell them in bulk to his contacts, he would sell them to customers who came into the shop.

It was hilarious; women would come in to buy a pound of mince and would leave with two pairs of boots, one for them and a bigger pair for their husbands. The cutting room became like a bloody changing room, there were people everywhere, trying on different sizes until they found the perfect fit. Word got round and people started coming from all over London to get a pair. Roy was shrewd and if a stranger came in to buy a pair, he would insist that they bought some meat as well. We sold the lot in under three weeks. The shops turnover also increased by over a thousand pounds. Another nice little earner.

We also had Lois Jeans. They were a Spanish make and were an "up market" Levi. Five thousand pairs arrived one Thursday morning. Roy and I unloaded the lorry, as always, there was much more than we expected, but of course Roy never said no. Roy's brother's lock up was used, as was my Dad's shed. The boxes had a mix of sizes and styles. There were about three thousand pairs of denim jeans and two thousand pairs of corduroy jeans. The corduroys were more expensive and extremely popular. They were a straight leg style, which were the height of fashion at the time.

These jeans retailed for a lot of money and were "the" jeans to be seen in. I remember my sister and her mates being really excited that we had Lois jeans because they were only sold in the trendiest of shops.

Roy (stupidly) thought he could do the same again and sell them to the shop customers. This proved to be a nightmare. Boots were easy to shift, everyone knows what shoe size they are, but jeans are a completely different ball game. You have different leg sizes, waist sizes, styles etc. People would come in and end up trying on five pairs before they bought any. You could also only have one person at a time in the cutting room trying them on. Every time I went out to restock the window display, there would be a half-naked person trying on bloody jeans. Still, it did have its plus side, a lot of the buyers were Mums and their teenage daughters.

After a week, Roy abandoned the idea and decided to sell them on in bulk. Gaz wanted his money and Roy was running out of time.

My girlfriend at the time had an uncle who lived in Bethnal Green. We were due to babysit for them that night. His name was Colin. He was a big, no nonsense east ender. I liked him as soon as I met him; he was a bit of a "jack the lad", late twenties and worked in the docks. While he was waiting for his wife to get ready, I asked him if he wanted any Lois Jeans. He laughed and said "Not the same ones that have just been on Police 5?" (A popular crime show at that time). I nodded and gave him a wink. Ten minutes later we were in Colin's car on our way to the shop and the babysitting had gone out of the window. This was much more important. Colin wanted a thousand pairs and was confident of selling them in the docks.

Roy took a chance with Colin, bearing in mind he had never met the guy before. He shook hands and let Colin drive away with a thousand pairs of expensive Lois Jeans. The gamble paid off because within a week, Colin had paid Roy and took another five hundred pairs.

The East End docks had practically closed down back then. Just a few boats now and again were unloaded. Containers had replaced them and these were being unloaded at Tilbury and Felixstowe, so although Colin couldn't get much gear himself, he was always able to "shift" a load here and there. He was a popular guy with lots of contacts. These contacts were all looking to earn a few bob on the side, so if Colin took a thousand pairs of jeans, he probably gave ten contacts one hundred pairs each. These contacts in turn then gave them to another ten contacts and suddenly the whole lot were sold and everyone made a small profit.

Roy and Colin became firm friends and he would prove to be a great contact for Roy in months to come.

But the biggest plus about meeting Colin was that he introduced Roy to two of his friends. They were cousins "Teddy and Danny" (I never knew their last names and I'm not sure if Roy ever did). All we knew at the time was that they were from "The Island".

For those not familiar with East London, "The Island" means the Isle of Dogs. Although called an Island, it's only surrounded by water on 3 sides. There's a few theories as to how it got its name. Some say it's because Edward XI used to let his greyhounds roam there, but others say it's because it was mainly marshland hundreds of years ago and there were large colonies of water birds, so it was called the Isle of Ducks and over the years Ducks became Dogs. Locals say it's because anyone forced to live there led a Dog's Life.

The main thing to know was that it was a "hard" place to live. You had to be hard to survive living there. Teddy and Danny pretty much "ran" the Island. These were proper gangsters. The real thing. I had never met anyone that carried a gun before. These guys did.

They were not big in size but they had a presence about them that commanded respect. And they absolutely loved Roy.

Roy was impressed when he was introduced to them because they seemed to know all about him. He was simply known in the East End as "The Butcher". Over the past year or so if something went missing, a lorry was hi-jacked or something appeared in the papers about stolen goods, apparently London villians would say something like "I bet the Butchers involved."

Roy loved the admiration especially when it came from two well-known gangsters.

The first time I met them was when they came to the shop early one day. They were dressed immaculately in tailored mohair suits, they didn't have a hair out of place and looked like film stars. They took one look at me and said "Ah you must be the Butcher Boy, we've heard a lot about you son."

So, that was it. From then on Roy was "The Butcher" and I was known as the "Butcher Boy".

Roy was gaining notoriety all the time. He himself had become a "face". He had Gaz and his team that could get anything, Mr. Patel had the cash to buy most things, Colin had enough contacts to distribute through the East End and now he had the Cousins to back him up with muscle if needed. It was a perfect little "firm."

What could possibly go wrong? The shops were making money and the deals were getting bigger and bigger.

Chapter 15

New Boys

Stevie, like me, had been with Roy since he left school at sixteen. There was always banter in the shop between the three of us, normally good humoured and we were forever taking the piss out of each other. There were constant egg fights, which normally ended up with me getting the worse of it, or we'd lock each other in the chiller or freezer and then turn out the lights (very scary).

But Stevie could be very moody as well. If he had a row with his girlfriend, which he did frequently, he would be in a foul mood all day. No amount of banter or jokes could knock it out of him.

He had been spending a couple of days a week over at the Plaistow shop until Roy was confident that the staff there could be trusted. The Plaistow shop was always busy; the deli counter was extremely popular in the area as was the grocery side which Roy had now grown into a nice bit of business. A lot of the knocked off stuff Roy could now sell through the Plaistow shop. Roy was getting tea, coffee, sugar, baked beans even eggs from his network of delivery drivers and all were being sold in the shop.

Stevie worked at the Plaistow shop for about 6 months before returning to East Ham full time. Roy had got to know the staff better during that time and made Ginger Pete (no prizes for guessing how he got his name), the new shop manager.

So Stevie was back, it was just like old times: "The three Amigos".

While Stevie had been away, Roy had started a part timer. He was an old retired butcher who lived locally. He came in two or three times a week between midday until closing.

Now because Stevie was used to being in charge over at Plaistow he returned to the shop a different person. He was constantly arguing with Roy over decisions involving the shop. They would argue about the window display, orders, pricing, basically everything. To Roy, he had become a pain in the arse.

There was an atmosphere in the shop that wasn't healthy, and then suddenly it all kicked off. Roy asked Stevie to do something, Stevie ignored him, Roy asked him again and Stevie just walked away. There was a lot of shouting and swearing, Stevie tore off his white coat and said he was leaving and not coming back. Roy said good riddance and that was that.

True to his word, Stevie never stepped foot in the shop again. He left in September 1975 with the sound of "Sailing" by Rod Stewart playing on the radio.

So now it was just me, Roy and the old part timer. Christmas was just around the corner and we needed to get some staff in quickly. Roy got one of the butchers from the Plaistow shop to come over full time and then asked me to find us a new "Saturday boy". It was like a promotion; I was now the number two in the shop and would be left to run things whilst Roy was out doing his skullduggery.

Instead of taking on one Saturday boy I took on two. Stevies's younger brother, Fred, came in after school to help clear up, but couldn't do Saturdays because he was one of the best footballers of his age in the area and played for a number of teams at weekends. The official Saturday boy was Davey. They were both fifteen.

We became a well-oiled machine. Roy would be around early in the mornings to help with preparation, then at about 11am he would be out and about. I would be left to run the shop until he came back later in the day. The other butcher would cut and serve during the day, the part timer came in around midday for a few hours and then Fred would turn up around 4pm to help clear up.

This also meant that it was me who dealt with any deals that turned up during the day. Roy always made sure there was a stash of cash in the shop so that I could buy anything that came in. A lot of the delivery drivers never met Roy, they would come in and just assume that I was "The Butcher" because it was me that said yes and agreed a price for what they had. I had become a younger version of Roy.

I was still only seventeen, but now had responsibility for running a small business on a day to day basis. I was earning terrific money from the different deals that we had going on, I very rarely touched my wages and had started to put a bit away every week for the future. I was going out every night of the week, either with Roy to the dogs or to clubs in the area. I got a cab everywhere and was always the first one up at the bar buying the drinks. Life was good, very good.

Surely, I thought, this was going to last forever?

Chapter 16

Old Ken and The Vouchers

The cousins, Teddy and Danny, became very familiar faces at the shop. Just like Gaz they were even there when I turned up at 07.00 in the morning. They would be wearing their made to measure suits, gangster overcoats and hand- made Italian shoes. I'm sure that they had just come from a club or late night drinking den somewhere. They were both around five feet ten inches tall and quite stocky. Teddy was the better looking of the two, with jet black hair all greased back and a side parting. Danny had the greased black hair as well but no parting, just combed all over from front to back. He also had a rather nasty looking scar that went from his left eyebrow down to the top of his left ear. Although it stood out and everyone noticed it, it was never mentioned.

It was as if they didn't want to miss anything, they wanted to be involved right from the start. They knew that Roy could earn them money and they didn't want to miss out on any of it. But that wasn't the only reason, Roy was simply great fun to be around, he had a "larger than life" personality, nothing seemed to get him down, and he always had a smile on his face. He made them feel good.

They were always talking about some scam or other and quite often there would be plans written on scraps of paper on the cutting blocks. But in September 1975 they decided to slow down a bit.

Gaz was always a bit paranoid. One day he turned up and was convinced he had been followed from his house in Dagenham all the way to the shop in East Ham. Roy laughed and told him it was just his imagination. Then the cousins turned up, and they said that there was a car parked across the road with two guys sitting in it who appeared to be watching the shop. Definitely old bill. So the four of them decided it was time to slow down a bit, have a cooling off period for three months.

Over the past eighteen months or so we had managed to shift everything that had turned up, no matter what quantity. From eight tons of corned beef to a lorry load of sanitary towels. Everyone was still earning good money from some of the smaller scams so there was no need to risk everything by going for the elusive "big one". They all shook hands and agreed to meet up again in January. If the old bill were following any of them they would certainly get fed up if nothing much happened in three months. They just wouldn't have the man power to stick it out.

So Roy decided to concentrate once again on the deliveries. The records and tapes no longer came into the shop, they went straight to Meads and Roy just took his cut (so did I). Deliveries always went round the back and no one took much notice of deliveries being made to a small parade of shops.

However, Roy had become friendly with an old shopkeeper called Ken. I say old; he was only about fifty but he had silver hair which made him look older than his years. He had one of those typical corner shops on a local council estate. He was always open and sold everything.

Old Ken mentioned to Roy one day about a nice little earner he had going. Of course Roy's ears pricked up straightaway. Old Ken said he had a couple of housewives in the Barking area that did leaflet delivery. They lived on his estate and one day approached him to ask if he wanted any vouchers.

These ladies delivered small booklets of grocery vouchers. They would put them through the doors of people on the estate. In the booklet there would be maybe eight or ten vouchers. Maybe two pence off a jar of Nescafe or four pence off Margarine. People cut these vouchers out of the booklets and took them to their local Grocers and exchanged them for the goods. So if a jar of Nescafe was twenty five pence, they would hand over a two pence voucher and twenty three pence in cash. Simple. The shop owner then takes the vouchers to a cash and carry and exchanges them for more coffee and gets his money refunded. The cash and carry get their money back from their suppliers. The system works, sales of coffee go up and everyone wins.

Now these ladies were selling Old Ken a few hundred booklets a week. Booklets may be worth twenty five pence in vouchers; Ken would buy them at ten pence each. But he would get the full value back from the cash and carry.

Roy wanted to try this out to see if it worked, cos if it did, he wanted some of it. He bought fifty books from Old Ken for fifteen pence each, came back to the shop and we all stood around ripping out the vouchers from the booklets. Each booklet had thirty two pence of vouchers in them, so sixteen pounds in value. Roy had paid seven pounds fifty for them. He got in the van and drove off to a cash and carry in Dagenham. He bought some coffee, sugar and tea. He handed over the vouchers and the girl agreed they were worth sixteen pounds and Roy just paid the balance. It worked. This was like buying money. But of course for Roy this had to be bigger. Much, much bigger.

Roy was like a big kid. He'd just earnt eight pound fifty, which was nothing to him but it was the sheer potential of it. "Fuck hi-jacking lorries, this little scam is genius." He was like a dog with two dicks.

He made a phone call to the local unemployment office; he said that his wife was looking for a bit of part time work, as the kids were getting a bit older. He had noticed some local woman delivering leaflets and thought that would suit his wife perfectly. The nice helpful lady on the phone gave him a number to call. June was the local co-coordinator for leaflet drops in his area. Roy went to visit June, when he came back he said there were leaflets everywhere. They were in every room, on each stair, in the kitchen, everywhere. Now I don't know what Roy said or did but within days he was going out and coming back with thousands of booklets. Sometimes, as many as five thousand at a time. He was obviously paying June a nice few quid (I think he may have been giving her something extra as well, if you know what I mean). Every spare minute we had we were cutting vouchers out of these booklets, screwing them up a bit so they looked used and putting them in hundred pound piles. There were piles everywhere.

Roy worked this scam in many ways. He would either take a thousand pounds worth of vouchers to Mr. Patel. Mr. Patel would give him seven hundred pounds cash. Mr. Patel was happy because he was getting three hundred pounds for nothing as he would claim the whole amount back from the manufacturer. Roy was giving June about two hundred pounds, so he was making five hundred quid every time. Some weeks he could do this three or four times. When it got a bit heavy, Mr. Patel would tell Roy to slow down for a week or two. Roy would simply go to another cash and carry and buy goods with them. He would then sell these goods to his network of local shop keepers. He just couldn't lose. We even took on one of Roy's younger cousins just to come in a few hours a day to cut out coupons!

It lasted for months; we all made a shed load of money. Then there was a massive clamp down. Mr. Patel called Roy one day and said that he had just had a visit from Limehouse CID, asking why his cash and carry was the biggest receiver of vouchers in the whole of the UK? Mr. Patel did his usual (pretended not to speak much English and just kept shrugging his shoulders), and eventually they left. But Roy shut down the operation there and then. No more vouchers.

Ever wondered why you stopped getting these type of things through the door or why they stopped appearing in Daily Newspapers? Well, Roy had a big hand in it.

So we had Gaz being followed, the shop being watched and now Mr Patel visited by CID. Coincidence?

But as usual it was all easy come and easy go for Roy. There would always be something else just around the corner and Roy always made money. Or so he thought…

Chapter 17

Black Ties, Big Mouths

I remember one night out with Roy and the Cousins; it was for a "black tie" boxing do. I didn't know what that meant and had to ask Roy.

"You've got to wear a dicky bow and a penguin suit."

The thought didn't thrill me.

"I'll look a complete wanker."

Roy just laughed.

"Listen, you've got to get one cos everyone will be wearing one. We'll all look wankers together."

He told me to go into Barking and see Jack Bunney, an old fashioned tailor and he'd sort me out.

I tried one on. I was right. I did look like a complete wanker. I can still remember the man in the shop asking me if I wanted a cumberbund, I thought he was offering me some kind of sexual experience and told him that I already had a girlfriend. I hired it.

Anyway, back to the black tie do. It was at York Hall in Bethnal Green; a famous East End boxing venue, and the Cousins had a table for ten. It was a three course meal and ours was obviously the best table in the room. We were so close to the ring that if any boxer's nose bled, it would have dripped onto our table.

There were the Cousins of course, me, Roy, a couple of East End publicans, a local councillor and a larger than life character called Richard. Richard owned two men's clothes shops, one in Romford and one in Upminster. He arrived in a red Rolls Royce and was very quickly the life and soul of the party.

The waiter came up and asked what we wanted to drink. There was no draught beer for sale so it was just bottles of Heineken. We all decided to have bottles of beer, and Richard shouted out to the waiter.

"It's my round; bring us a case of Heineken."

Five minutes later the waiter returned with a case of beer containing twenty four bottles. He put the case beside Richard and went to walk away, Richard grabbed him by his sleeve.

"Where you going?"

"Sorry Sir?"

"Where's the rest of it?"

"That is it Sir. You asked for a case."

Richard shook his head.

"No you wanker, a case each!"

Then he roared with laughter as did everyone else.

Sure enough, the waiter went away and kept coming back until each person had a case of beer beside them.

Now you have to understand that these guys were all trying to "out do" each other. They all had plenty of money and were keen to spend it. After the first bout, one of the cousins, Danny, stood up and asked if anyone would like to join him in a scotch. Everyone cheered and agreed that a Scotch would go down well. He called the waiter over.

"Okay, mate, we'll all have a scotch."

"Large ones Sir?"

"No you dipstick, a bloody bottle each of course!"

The waiter looked dumbfounded. But went away and came back with a case of Bells whiskey, a bottle for each of us. This went on all night, by the end of the evening I was sitting with a bottle of whisky, vodka, gin, bacardi and brandy and god knows how many beers.

We decided we should vote for the best boxer of the night and give him all the bottles that we had accumulated. Imagine the kids face when we presented him with over thirty bottles of different spirits.

His mum and dad came over and thanked us; his dad said something about struggling to get it home as they had come on the bus. Quick as a flash Teddy put his hand in his pockets and pulled out a ten pound note.He called the waiter over.

"Get these people a cab will you mate and make sure the cabbie takes all the booze as well."

As I said before, the Cousins were pure class.

Richard had a word with Roy about jeans.

"If you get any jeans mate, I'll have the lot. I can shift them through the shops."

Now this was a dangerous thing to say to Roy because he would now place an order with Gaz. The boys would go to work and get them. Next day Roy put the wheels in motion. Sure enough within two weeks Gaz was on the phone.

"Got the Jeans you wanted Roy, Levis, usual quantity, about five thousand pairs."

This was great news for Roy. Roy made the call to Richard. I heard the tone of his voice change when he was on the phone.

"What do you mean, you'll have fifty pairs? I've got you fucking five thousand!"

The problem was, Richard had no idea he was dealing with professionals. He could talk big, but when it came down to it he just didn't have the means to take this amount. He was also going through a divorce which was costing him a fortune.

Gaz turned up with the jeans later that day. Roy said he would get rid of them as usual but explained to Gaz about Richard.

"No problem Roy, let me go and have a quiet chat with him and tell him how these thing work. He'll soon change his mind."

Roy knew what this meant. Gaz would go and threaten him and then have someone beat him up or even worse.

Now, Roy was a criminal, no two ways about it, but he wasn't into getting people beaten up or maimed. He told Gaz not to worry and he would have his money in a few days. He had no idea how he could get rid of them. He had flooded the market with jeans just a few months before and no one really wanted any more. Certainly not five thousand pairs of the fuckers! He paid Gaz five pounds a pair for them out of his own money. So he coughed up twenty five grand. He ended up selling them on for ten, just to get rid of them. He lost fifteen thousand pounds on the deal.

Richard's name was never mentioned again. He never went to any more events with Roy or the Cousins. He got divorced, sold both his shops in Essex and moved to Australia later that same year. I think he knew he had upset some serious people.

Chapter 18

Hackney Birds and Bloody Noses

Towards the end of 1975, Mum and Dad went off to Cornwall for a couple of weeks, so I had the house to myself. They were going to leave in the early hours of Saturday morning. On the Friday before they left, me and Stuart met two girls from Hackney at a local nightclub. They were good fun, they both lived in a tower block somewhere near the old dog track, and we took them home, had a kiss, cuddle and fumble on the stairs and eventually left them at five in the morning. Before we said goodbye to them they mentioned a Football Club do that night at the Connaught Club just by the dog track, and they invited us to come along. We agreed.

 I decided to go straight to work. It was too late to go home anyway and Mum and |Dad would have already left for Cornwall so I got to the shop at six. Roy was already setting out the window display. He looked at me when I walked in still in my "going out" clothes and guessed what had happened.

"Well, well, well, if it isn't Mister Casanova himself, get your leg over last night did you?"

"Something like that Roy, I'll put the kettle on."

While I made a cup of tea Roy went over to the bakers and got four rolls. He came back and put some thick slices of ham in them. By twenty past six we were eating rolls and drinking tea.

"Bet you needed that. Good sort was she?"

We both laughed and got on with the display. The other butcher came in just before seven, surprised to see me already there.

"What did you do, shit the bed or something?"

Roy decided to interrupt.

"No, got his leg over some bird from Hackney."

They kept teasing me all morning.

"Best get yourself checked out mate, or wash your cock in dettol, you know what dirty birds those Hackney girls are."

They both thought it was great fun and kept the banter up all day. They even told most of the customers. Roy would be serving someone and then suddenly say something like "Ask Joe why he's got a smile on his face this morning."

I left the shop at four as usual, went home had a couple of hours kip then got ready to go out again at seven. I met Stuart in our favourite pub, had a pint and then got a cab to the Football Club.

We arrived at this shady downbeat club just after eight. The two girls from the previous night were standing at the bar. They waived and we walked over.

There was a palpable atmosphere in the club. There were groups of young guys standing around, and they all looked like they were expecting something to happen.

Stuart said he needed a piss and walked off towards the toilets, I got the beers in and continued talking to the girls. It was then that I noticed a group of six or seven guys follow Stuart into the toilets. I realised what was going to happen. I ran across the dance floor and entered the gents just in time to see Stuart fall to the ground from a punch by some much older guy. Two others thought it would be fun to kick him while he was on the floor. I lunged at the guy who had given Stuart a smack and caught him on the side of the head. We both fell to the floor, all I remember after that was being kicked and punched about the body and head. I must have passed out for a while.

When I came to, Stuart was on the floor next to me and there were two guys crouching over him asking him if he was okay. We both stood up, I had various cuts and bruises but not as bad as Stuart. He had a large cut on his head and blood was pouring down his face. We made our way out of the club and walked the short distance to the dog track, and from there we got a cab to East Ham memorial hospital. Stuart had eleven stitches to the cut on his head and I had three to a cut over my left eye.

So on Monday morning I arrived at the shop at seven, looking like I'd just gone ten rounds with Rocky Marciano. When I got there Roy was having a cup of tea with the cousins.

"Fuck me, what happened to you?"

"Bit of an altercation on Saturday night at a football club in Hackney, seems me and Stuart chose the wrong birds to go with."

The elder cousin, Danny, wanted to know more.

"Got any names?"

"No, just that we were at the Connaught club near the dog track, met a couple of birds and then about half a dozen guys jumped us in the toilets."

"I know that club well. Let me find out what I can."

They finished their tea and left. Roy told me to fuck off home and get some rest, Mondays we only opened for half a day anyway so I wouldn't be missed. I didn't argue, I could do with the sleep.

I went back to work on Tuesday as usual. My eye was still sore but the bruising around my nose and cheek had started to go down. At midday the shop phone rang, Roy answered it. He said a few words then put down the receiver. He called me over.

"Take the van and go to a pub on the Island called The George. It's just over the blue bridge as you enter the Island, the Cousins want to see you."

"When?"

"Now!"

I hadn't passed my test yet and was still having driving lessons but took the van anyway and made my way to the George. It was a traditional East End boozer, even at half past twelve it was busy, full of smoke and noise. Sitting at a table in the corner was Danny. He called me over. I sat down.

"Got some news for you about the bust up on Saturday. It's a little crew called the Donovans. Seems that Billy Donovan had his eye on Stuart's little bird and took offence that two outsiders were getting some of her attention."

I wasn't quite sure what to say.

"Okay."

As I spoke, the bar door opened and in walked Teddy and by the scruff of the neck he was holding Billy Donovan. They walked over and Teddy told Billy to sit down. I noticed that Billy had a bruise on the left side of his face. Good, I had caught him after all.

But I still wasn't sure what was happening. Did they want us to fight it out, was I supposed to punch the guy there and then? I wasn't sure what my next move should be. Danny spoke first. He looked at Billy.

"See this boy here, do you know who he is?"

"No Danny."

"He's the fucking Butcher Boy, that's who the fuck he is, and you, you little toe rag, are fucking lucky you're still breathing, cos he could have come after you and cut you up, but we talked him out of it."

"Thank you Danny."

Billy Donovan was actually shaking.

"He's part of our firm is the Butcher Boy and you know what happens to people who fuck with our firm, don't you?"

"Yes Danny, sorry Danny."

"Good. So I want you to shake his hand and apologise, cos, if you don't, I will allow him to cut you up, understand?"

Billy stuck out his hand, I pretended to be reluctant to shake it but finally agreed, and we shook hands."

Danny gave him a whack around the back of the head.

"Now go and get us all a beer and a scotch chaser. Look lively."

Billy did what he was told, came back with a tray containing four pints and four scotches.

Billy looked at me properly for the first time, then quietly said.

"I'm sorry mate, didn't know you were with the Cousins, anything you need, anytime, just let me know, okay?"

I nodded.

We finished our drinks. Danny looked at Billy.

"You still here?"

"Sorry Danny, I'm going now."

Billy Donovan left the pub, the Cousins started laughing. Teddy spoke for the first time.

"Good, been waiting for an excuse to frighten the shit out of that little firm. They needed to know who's in charge and now they know. You okay with everything Joe?"

"Yeah cheers, glad it's all settled."

Danny put his arm around me.

"Listen, I wasn't fucking joking with Billy Donovan, you *are* part of the firm, you and Roy. We all look after each other."

I thanked them both once again, left the pub, got in the van and drove very slowly back to the shop. When I got back, Roy already knew what had happened. He just looked at me and said.

"Sorted?"

I replied. "Yep all sorted."

We got back to work and it was never mentioned again. By the time mum and dad got back from Cornwall two weeks later, my face was back to normal ant the cut had virtually healed. They never knew what had happened.

Chapter 19

The BMT

As I said before we had many "characters" that came into the shop. One of these was Black Mickey the Thief.

He was known as Black Mickey because we knew many other Mickeys. There was a Mickey in the betting shop, a Mickey in the pub, and a couple of the regular customers were called Mickey Also, because he was the only one that was black.

To keep it easy we called him BMT, as in, Black Mickey the Thief.

He was a big man, probably 6ft 4inches tall, around eighteen stone and his face was lined with scars. He was also a bully.

But Roy being from hard-core east end dealt with him in the only way he could. He bullied the bully.

BMT would come into the shop having just robbed a shop or stolen a car and taken the stereo out and demand that Roy buy it. Roy would have none of it.

"Fuck off Mickey, bring me something I want and I'll buy it. If not just fuck off."

This would go on day after day, Mickey would bring in two car stereos and Roy wouldn't buy them because he didn't want them. BMT would scream and shout and then Roy would put on an act and tell him to fuck off. It happened practically every day until Mickey brought in something that Roy wanted, like watches or jewellery.

Roy once said to BMT. "If I'm not here, the boy's in charge, don't fuck about with him cos you'll deal with me later. Okay?"

Mickey agreed. I have to admit to being a bit apprehensive. Roy was spending more time out of the shop and there was this enormous black man demanding money every other day. I was only seventeen.

Roy said to me "If BMT comes in, be strong with him or he'll walk all over you. Remember you're the guvnor, you're in charge, you tell him how it's gonna be."

Luckily I remembered those words. On a black and dreary Wednesday sometime near the end of 1975 the BMT came into the shop. He had a holdall with him. Inside the holdall were two car stereos, a cassette player and a cheap watch.

"Give me thirty quid and you can have the lot"

The BMT was inches from my face.

"Okay, let's have a look Mickey and I'll see."

I looked in the bag and didn't think it was worth it.

"No thanks Mick, I'll swerve this time."

"What you fucking talking about man, each car system is worth a ton, give us twenty five and we'll call it quits."

I remembered Roy's words.

"Look Mickey we don't want it so fuck off and get us something we do want."

The BMT was angry. Here was a thirty year old man being told to fuck off by a seventeen year old kid, he didn't take it well.

"Don't fuck with me man, there's a bundle to be made with this lot, now give me a score and I'll move on."

"Fuck off Mickey, no way."

He punched the wall and I could see his knuckles start to go red.

I picked up one of the large steak knives, just in case.

He saw me and went for another angle. The sympathy angle. He spoke softly.

"Look Joe, if you don't want these I'll get you something else tomorrow, but today how about you lend me twenty quid, just between the two of us, Roy need never know."

Roy had a rule. Never, ever, lend money to anyone.

"Fuck off Mickey, get me something I want and then you'll have your cash."

Although I was frightened by this massive black man, Roy's words were ringing in my ears, "Do not show weakness, ever."

He threw the bag at me.

"You want something, do you? Okay, I'll go fucking get it. Give me one of your carrier bags."

I gave him a plain white plastic bag.

Outside the shop was a bus stop. Buses going to Barking town centre stopped there, and it was only a five minute journey to the station.

BMT ran out of the shop and jumped right onto a number 87 bus heading into Barking town centre.

I took no notice and carried on with my work. A few customers came in and I served them. Roy was unlikely to be back for another few hours.

Roughly half an hour later, possibly sooner, a bus pulled up on the other side of the road outside the pub, I saw the BMT jump off and run across the road into the shop. He was carrying our plastic bag. He looked at me and threw the bag across the counter.

"Here you are, you cunt, now give me fifty quid for that lot."

I very slowly opened the bag. Inside were several watches, various gold chains, some diamond rings and about ten pair of gold earrings. I tried to play it cool.

"Okay then, fifty quid for the lot but I'll keep the car stereos as well."

BMT took the money and left. I didn't know the whole story until a few days later. The local paper was delivered and on the front page was the headline "Smash and Grab at Fishers". Fishers was an up market jewellery store in Barking. It was on the station parade. This is what had happened.

BMT left me at the shop and jumped on a bus going into Barking town Centre. He got off the bus at the train station, walked straight over to the building site opposite, picked up a brick, calmly walked across the road and threw it through the jewellers window. He grabbed as much as he could and put it into the plastic bag and walked away. He then jumped on another bus that brought him back to the shop.

When Roy returned later that day I showed him the jewellery.

"Fuck me mate this is worth a few bob."

I took a diamond ring for my sister for her forthcoming birthday and a few gold chains. Roy did the same. We sold the rest for a hundred quid to Roy's brother Frank who dabbled in bits of gold.

BMT would come and go, he could be in the shop every day for a month, trying to sell odds and sods. Then he'd disappear for three months or so, due to having to spend a bit of time at Her Majesty's pleasure. That was the way he led his life, but he was always as mad as fuck.

Chapter 20

Christmas 1975

Christmas 1975 would prove to be our busiest yet, and although Roy had been concentrating on his "other activities", he realised that this was his bread and butter. Christmas was a time when he would make serious money. No point in taking his eye off the ball, if, god forbid, everything fell apart, he would still make a living from butchery.

He had a bit of a shock when he tried to make his normal turkey order with the Norfolk farmer. He had sold up and his farm was being turned into a new golf course. This was a blow; Roy had been going there for a few years now and had to quickly find another supplier. He found one in Dunmow in Essex. The only problem was this one didn't deliver; we would have to collect them ourselves. We agreed to pick them up ten days before Christmas Eve.

Now that Stevie was no longer around it would be me and Roy that went to collect them. We needed about two hundred and fifty that year.

We arrived at the farm around 09.00am on a cold, wet, frosty Sunday morning. It looked like a bomb site. There was old farm machinery everywhere; there must have been ten dogs running wild and just as many cats. The whole place smelt of dog shit and dead poultry.

The farmer, Reg, met us and began to tell us where to go for the turkeys. Dunmow wasn't a million miles away from East London, but he might as well have been speaking Chinese! He looked like a tramp and his accent was like one of the bad southerners from the film "Deliverance".

We got the gist and followed him to a barn about two hundred yards away. He walked in front and we followed him in the transit van. It was like a scene from the Pied Piper, with us and all the animals all following this strange man.

When we entered the barn, it stank, as you would expect. It was full of dead turkeys that had been killed the day before and then hung up by their feet. Some had been plucked but the majority hadn't. Roy had agreed with old Reg that we would pay by the pound for our turkeys. So roughly two hundred and fifty at an average of twelve pounds per bird was around three tonnes. This was twice the weight that the transit was legally able to take but, as usual, Roy was confident that if we took it slowly on the ride home we would be ok.

Suddenly to both our amazement, old Reg walked off. He said something about helping ourselves and let him know when we had finished. Surely he didn't trust me and Roy to weigh and count our own turkeys? But that was exactly what happened. In the barn was an old table and next to it were some big scales. We pulled the transit up to the scales and just started throwing turkeys in the back, sod weighing them and having to pay for them. When we got to thirty we stopped. Okay, now to start counting and weighing.

When we'd counted our two hundred turkeys, Roy said "Okay, let's put a few more on for free". So we put on another twenty. This meant we now had our 250, but only 200 had been weighed. The actual weight of the two hundred Turkeys was two thousand six hundred pounds. We decided that we should only pay for two thousand two hundred pounds. We went and found old Reg and told him the total weight was two thousand two hundred pounds in weight and we paid him. He seemed happy enough. So, not only did we have fifty free turkeys, we also had four hundred pounds in weight that we hadn't paid for. Result.

What we actually had in total weight was about three and half ton of turkeys. This was now nearly three times the legal weight that the transit should carry. Roy started her up and we crawled to the barn doors, second gear was about all she could manage. In the rear view mirror we suddenly saw Reg running towards us waiving his arms in the air and shouting at us to stop.

"Fuck it." said Roy "I think he's rumbled us." We were going so slow we had no choice but to stop the van. Reg told us to stay where we were and not go any further. Then he disappeared back in the Barn.

"Fuck it Roy, what if he's gone to get his shotgun or something? You know what these country people are like, he'll probably shoot us and bury us in his field."

Reg came out of the barn, with a massive smile on his face and holding the two biggest turkeys I had ever seen. They weighed about thirty pounds each.

"Theree go boyz, one each. Merry Christmas."

We thanked the farmer for his kindness, then, Roy turned to me and under his breath said.

"Fuck me, that's all we need, more fucking turkeys."

We waived him goodbye and said we'd see him next year. Now the problem was getting the transit back to East London. We were going down the A12 at about twenty five miles an hour in third gear, praying that we'd make it. Smoke had started to appear from the bonnet and there was a grinding noise coming from the back wheels. Then our worst nightmare. Blue lights behind us. A police car was flashing us to stop.

We pulled over and Roy got out and walked towards the police car. As always he had a big smile on his face. I just sat there thinking the worst. I heard the back doors open, raised voices and then laughing.

I looked into the side mirror and couldn't believe what I was seeing. Two policeman walking back to their car each carrying a massive turkey. Roy had given them the turkeys that old Reg had just given us. They got in their car and pulled up alongside us.

"Okay Roy, take it easy mate, drive slowly. Good luck."

I couldn't believe it. Was their nothing that this man couldn't get away with?

We drove slowly and it took us another two hours to get back to the shop. The poor van had to be fitted with a new gearbox and back axel two weeks later. But we had got away with over a ton of fresh turkey.

It was as we had thought - our busiest Christmas ever. Long hours, hard work, but great rewards.

I started to wonder what 1976 would bring.

Chapter 21

1976 and Me

I think for all of us there is one year in our lives that stands out from any other. For me, that year was 1976. I was just eighteen.

It was the year that I passed my butchery exams. I passed with honours and was now a fully- fledged master butcher. For me the course was a piece of piss. Roy (and Stevie) were the best teachers ever. There wasn't a piece of meat that I didn't know name of, how to cut it, what to do with it and even how to cook it. The theory side (biology and meat technology) interested me and so I just soaked it up.

It was also the year that I passed my driving test. I paid my driving instructor with meat instead of cash (naturally), and twice a week he would drive away with a leg of lamb, some chops and mince. Roy said it was his treat.

I started to save a bit of money every week with a local building society. Some weeks I was putting away as much as three hundred pounds, depending on how much skullduggery Roy had been up to. I walked in one day with my girlfriend. I heard the man behind the counter say to one of his colleagues. "Here they come again. Bonny and Clyde."

I went ballistic. I asked him to repeat what he said and what he meant by it. He kept apologising over and over again. I told him he should keep his mouth shut and then closed the account there and then. I took every penny in cash and opened up a new account with another building society just up the road.

It was the year that I had my first holiday abroad, two weeks in Benidorm with my best mate Stuart. I had met Stuart a year before. He was very much like me and had a few things going on the side. He worked at a local paint factory and helped load the lorries. Of course he managed to put on a few "extras" for his favourite drivers and they would square him up at the end of the week. To be honest a fair amount of this "extra" paint ended up in a certain butchers shop in East Ham. Like me he very rarely touched his wages and he was always up for a laugh. So the two of us would go out every night until silly o'clock but would always be at work by seven the next morning. There were days when we both decided it was too late to go home so just went straight to work. You can do that when you're eighteen.

I had my suits hand made at a jewish tailors in Rathbone Market in Canning Town, the same tailors that the cousins used. It was also the tailor that Billy Walker (the ex- British Heavyweight Champion) used. I had a full length leather coat made as well. I must have looked like a man from the Gestapo. I spent fifty to sixty pounds on Italian leather shoes. Money was no problem.

It was also the first year that I started having regular sex (not just occasional bits and pieces). I started to notice a lot of attention from women, not girls, but women in their late twenties, thirties and even forties. As you can imagine it's mainly women who come into a butchers shop. They take their kids to school and then do their shopping. One such lady was a regular customer called Elaine who came into the shop every day. She was thirty two, had a couple of kids and lived about five minutes from the shop. She had long dark hair, a lovely figure and was overall very attractive. She came in one Monday morning and bought some bits and pieces and then with a smile asked if I could deliver it that afternoon. She also said that if I came round about 2pm she would make me a nice cup of tea. I smiled and said "Anything for you Elaine."

I got to her house at around 1.45pm; she opened the door wearing her dressing gown. "You're a bit early, I've just got out of the shower." She then grabbed me and we started kissing. We ended upstairs in her bedroom. I saw Elaine about twice a week for most of 1976.

I was a fit, strong, blond haired blue eyed young man with plenty of money. I oozed confidence and had the gift of the gab. I had become a mini Roy.

For me one of the most important things about 1976 was the music. Soul and Funk were being played in the clubs and this became "our" music. We were into Brass Construction, The Fatback Band, Ohio Players, Parliament and Heatwave. The DJ's at the time were, Chris Hill, Robbie Vincent, Big Tom Holland, and the late great Froggy.

Stuart and I travelled everywhere to see these guys play their sounds. Lacey Lady was the place to be on a Friday, but there was also Room at The Top, Circus Tavern, Lively Lady in Stratford and The Green Gate in Newbury Park. And the ultimate club on Saturdays was The Goldmine on Canvey Island.

We went everywhere by cab. Cost was no problem, public transport just didn't come into it. We wore the most fashionable clothes, had our ears pierced (left of course, didn't want to give the wrong impression).

Swing was being played at the Lacey and the Goldmine, and we all dressed up in 1940's clothes as American GIs and danced to the sounds of Glen Miller and Benny Goodman. We thought we were the nuts.

I was also spending a lot of time with Roy and the Cousins at the local dog track or horse racing. I remember overhearing them one day, when they were discussing a night out at the famous Venus

Steak House restaurant. "Don't forget to bring the boy with you." This meant a lot to me because it confirmed that I was part of the "firm".

I had, over the past couple of years become friendly with most of Roy's family. I would often go for a drink or a game of snooker with Roy's older brother Frank on a Monday or a Thursday afternoon, when we closed early. Or I would have a beer with Sidney, his younger brother. Sometimes the whole family would go out and of course I was invited.

I now felt that I had two families: my own of course, but I was now also part of Roy's family, the Marshall's.

Roy and I were like brothers.

Chapter 22

1976 and Roy

In stark contrast to mine, Roy's 1976 would be horrendous. It started well. Christmas had been a great earner and trade in both shops was brilliant in January and February.

The "cooling off" period finished at the end of January. The firm had a meeting and it was decided that they should all go back to normal. The deals started coming in fast and furious: a lorry load of tea had turned up and was dispatched very quickly through Mr. Patel and numerous other contacts. Colin and the Cousins were busy forging luncheon vouchers and this was a fantastic earner. It was like printing money but without the risk. Everyone took luncheon vouchers and you could buy almost anything with them. From fish and chip shops to grocers, if you saw the "LV" sign on the door, you were in. No one looked at them carefully because they were just luncheon vouchers, and only worth twenty five pence each. Roy was selling them to his contacts for fifteen pence each; he was paying only ten pence each for them so was making 5p a time. Not much, you might say, but when you're selling five hundred books of them and each book had a face value of five pounds, suddenly it's serious money.

The summer of 1976 was the hottest on record, and it started early and seemed to never end. Most days it was in the 90's. The problem was that people don't buy meat when it's hot. No one wants a nice Sunday roast when it's boiling hot outside, everyone has salads instead. We all knew this from experience but we weren't prepared for just how quiet it was. People didn't have barbecues back then and most of our customers didn't even have a back garden. Also, that summer there were talks about Fords going on strike (they eventually did in September). Most of our ladies' husbands worked at Fords and decided to make cut backs. Instead of buying chops or steaks, it was now just mince and sausages. Roy was losing money every week from the two shops, something that would have seemed impossible a year earlier. Something else had happened as well. Supermarkets.

In our area we had Victor Values and Wallis. These were the start of the supermarket chains. They sold everything, including meat, and were selling it cheaper than us. For the first time, people could go into one store and do their whole week's shopping.

But Roy was still spending big as usual. His bets were just as big, his wife was still buying the most expensive clothes, and the twins were kitted out with the best designer gear. Roy had just bought Sue a brand new Audi. So there were still big outgoings, but the incomings were not as large.

I noticed something change in Roy in 1976. Whereas before this had all been one big game, now it had become a burden. He now had to have the deals, where- as before he could take them or leave them.

He was made an offer for the Plaistow shop by a friend of Mr Patel. They wanted to convert three shops into a small supermarket. Roy decided to accept the offer and concentrate on the East Ham shop. He sold the Plaistow shop in September.

One other thing happened in 1976 that would suddenly make Roy wonder if all this skullduggery was worth all the effort.

Roy disappeared one day and came back two hours later with a transit van full of dresses.

There was nothing unusual about this of course; he was always turning up with something.

He'd been over to the Island to see the Cousins and while he was there one of their boys had turned up with some dresses.

We unloaded and put them onto hanging rails in the garage at the back of the shop. "Lovely gear," said Roy. "Designer by the look of it."

It certainly was designer. It was on its way to a fashion show in Manchester, and was pinched from a service station somewhere on the M1.

About an hour later we were listening to the radio when the news came on, and they mentioned that a vehicle had been stolen containing the entire collection for a fashion show in Manchester. This meant that the show couldn't go ahead unless the items were found because they were all unique.

"Fuck," was all Roy could say. He realised that this lot may be hard to shift as everyone would be looking for it.

Problem was, Roy had spent the last hour phoning everyone and telling them that he had loads of designer gear, and he'd even given the name of some of the designers.

Roy called Danny. "Have you heard the news about the dresses?" Danny was obviously laughing because Roy then said "Fuck me Dan, everyone's looking for the stuff and it's all in my fucking garage and I've just spent the last hour telling everyone I've got it."

They decided to keep the stuff in the garage for a while, until the heat died down, and not make any more calls. If anyone mentioned it, Roy was to say that it had all been gotten rid of. Hopefully this would put people off the scent and no one would come looking for it.

Later that day, two big guys walked into the shop and asked for Roy. I'd never seen these guys before and hearing a northern accent, I was a bit nervous about what to say. Luckily I didn't have to say a word. Roy came out and introduced himself, it was all smiles and handshakes, then Roy walked out the back of the shop and into the flat with the two big guys closely behind.

About fifteen minutes later I was at the back of the shop washing my hands next to the door that leads to the flat. The door opened and Roy's voice whispered "call the police," and then the door shut again.

I was stunned; those were three words that I thought Roy would never say. Was it a wind up? Probably not. I stood still for a full five minutes, not sure what to do. Then Roy appeared, his face white, and he looked in shock.

"Did you call them?"

"No mate, I wasn't sure what to do." I replied.

"Thank fuck for that," said Roy.

"What's going on Roy?"

"Those two blokes are fucking heavies from up north, they've come for the dresses, and I told them I didn't have them, then they pulled out guns and threatened to come back and shoot Sue and the kids if I don't give them the stuff back by 09.00 tomorrow."

Roy sat down on one of the butchers blocks and put his hands on either side of his face as though he was trying to think it through. I was in no doubt.

"Fuck it Roy, we should we call the police."

Roy was silent for a few seconds, then stood up.

"Bollocks, this is a job for the Cousins."

Roy made some calls to Teddy and Danny; they were at the shop within half an hour. A plan was made.

Roy told Sue when she came home that she would have to stay at her mum's that night as there was going to be major roadworks outside the shop, starting at 9pm that night. He told her that the council had been in touch and recommended that if possible, they should stay somewhere else that night as it would be noisy all through the evening. Roy said he would stay at the flat as he would have to be up early the next day to go down Smithfield Market. She believed him and went off to her mum's.

Teddy and Danny would stay the night at the shop with Roy, ready for when the northern guys turned up early the next morning.

I was still at the shop later when the cousins came back. They had two hand guns and two shot guns. They also had another guy with them. To this day, he's the biggest man I have ever seen. They called him Max. He was about 6ft 8in tall and built like a brick shit house. I had never seen anyone with arms that big before. He never spoke and his expression never changed all the time he was there. I left the shop at 9.00 that night. Roy asked me to come in early the next day and open the shop at 06.00. If it all turned ugly, I was to call the old bill. (He never told Teddy and Danny that bit.)

So off I went home. I don't think I got any sleep that night and got back to the shop at quarter to six the next morning. My heart was pounding.

I opened the shop, and began to work as usual. Everything was quiet from the flat. At about 07.00 Roy came out in his white coat and just said "Everything Okay?"

"Yep, all quiet," I said.

"If they come in the front of the shop, just act normal and call for me. I'll come out and take them out the back into the flat. Danny will be hiding in the kitchen and Teddy and Max are waiting on the stairs."

Roy then went back in the flat. Now you have to remember, I was only eighteen and it was now likely that I was about to witness a proper shoot out where people were going to either seriously injured or die. But I just carried on as normal. It's amazing how much my life had changed in those four years with Roy.

An hour later, the two guys from up north came into the shop; they smiled and asked for Roy, but just before I called out for him one of them said,

"So you're the Butcher Boy? Heard a lot about you."

I smiled and said "All good things I hope?"

The bigger one just said, "So far."

I called for Roy. He came out, they shook hands and then walked out into the flat and closed the door.

Then there was a lot of noise, shouting and swearing, and then all went quiet. I was waiting for a loud bang, but it never happened.

I continued to put the window display on.

Roy came out first, about forty five minutes later.

"Jesus Christ," he said. Then let out a laugh, but it was a very nervous laugh.

"Well?" was all I could think to say. "Where is everyone?"

"Teddy and Danny have loaded up the van with the dresses; the two heavies are taking them back to Manchester. Turns out there's a reward for their return of twenty five grand, and we've agreed to split it five ways. I've just made five thousand quid."

Then very quickly he added "Well, less a grand for you." Then we both started laughing.

Roy desperately needed a drink. He was shaking for the rest of the day. At about two o'clock, Roy and I disappeared across the road to the pub, leaving the shop to be run by the other two. He then told me the full story.

When he had walked into the flat with the two heavies, Max jumped from the stairs and grabbed one by the neck. Danny pounced on the other one, then Teddy came out of the kitchen with his shot gun pointed at them.

They gave up their guns and then all sat down in Roy's front room. It was all very calm. The bigger one of the guys said that they had been hired by a security firm to get the clothes back. If they got them back within forty eight hours they would get twenty five grand. The clothes were priceless as they were "one offs". Without them the fashion show couldn't go ahead and people were flying in from all over the world to be at attend it.

The bigger guy then went on to say that as soon as they were hired their first stop was always going to be the "Butcher." If he didn't have them there was a good chance that he would know who did. It seemed that even up north, Roy had a reputation.

The two northerners also knew of the Cousins. Their reputation was well known everywhere, so they knew they could be in trouble if they didn't strike a deal.

So, a deal was struck, and everyone was happy. The reward would be split five ways. Roy and the Cousins would get five grand each.

True to their word, five grand arrived four days later by motorcycle courier. Roy gave me a thousand pounds cash. We went to the dogs that night.

All ended well. But Roy was never quite the same after this incident. I think it was finally dawning on him just how dangerous this lifestyle could be and how it could affect Sue and the kids.

But there seemed to be no way out.

Chapter 23

Captured

It was Sunday, 10th October 1976; I was staying at my new girlfriend's house having just finished Sunday dinner with her and her mum and dad. It was just after five o'clock and we were about to start getting ready to go out. We were going to see Clint Eastwood's new film, The Outlaw Josey Wales.

Their phone rang and her dad answered it. "It's for you Joe, it's your dad".

There were no mobile phones back in 1976, so if I was going somewhere I would leave a number for mum and dad if they had to contact me in an emergency. This was obviously an emergency.

My first thought was that one of my grandparents had died. Granddad had been ill for some time so when I took the call from dad I was expecting some bad news.

Dad's voice was edgy.

"Get yourself home son. Roy's been captured, the old bill are searching the shop as we speak. You could be next. I've just got rid of anything that was lying around in the house. You do the same." He hung up.

I was in shock. I never, ever, thought that this could happen. As I have said before, everything seemed like one big game. Roy was invincible, he was the man. They couldn't capture Roy, not Roy. I stood silent for a moment, taking it all in. I needed to get going.

I had about thirty pairs of jeans in the boot of my car. I also had three cases of wine on the back seat. We had just had a delivery of wine the previous day.

I told my girlfriend that my Granddad had taken a turn for the worst and I had to go home straightaway. On the way home I dumped the jeans and the wine into the river Roding. I stopped the car down the end of a deserted road and threw the lot into the river. The lot was worth about three hundred pounds. Money didn't seem important anymore.

When I got home I expected to see police cars outside, but everything was very quiet. When I went in mum and dad were sitting there watching the TV.

Dad looked up. "Whatever was in the shed or the garage has now gone. I've dumped it."

It was only a few cases of this and that so no big deal really. "Okay dad. My car's clean if you know what I mean. So I suppose we just sit and wait?"

"Not much more we can do son." I wanted to go to the shop, but decided that was not a good idea. The old bill were probably still there. Dad said that Sue had called him about an hour earlier and said the police had taken Roy away and had a warrant for the flat. They had started searching it when she made the call. She had called us first then said she would call a solicitor for Roy. All the numbers that I needed were at the shop. I should call the Cousins and Gaz to let them know but I didn't have the numbers. I wasn't sure if Sue had either. It would all have to wait until the morning.

I didn't sleep at all that night. Every time I heard a sound or a car outside I was convinced it was the police. I got up at 4am and made a cup of tea. Dad heard me get up, so he got up as well and we sat together in the kitchen talking it through. He kept saying

"Remember, you're just the butcher boy, whatever has gone on in the shop, you know nothing about it. You're just a butcher."

I got to the shop at 5am. I opened up and set about putting in the window display. Business as usual. Sue came down from the flat about 6am and it was obvious she had been crying. I put my arms around her and she started crying again. I tried to tell her it would all be okay, but, to be honest, even I wasn't sure about that.

I asked her where the police had searched. She said just the flat and the garage at the back, but not the shop, they hadn't touched the shop. This was great news. We kept a large sum of money hidden in the shop and there was also a stash of jewellery and watches. I checked and they were still there.

 I asked her if she had called a solicitor, and she said she had, a close friend of hers had recommended one. Now I needed to make some calls. I tried both the Cousins. No answer. I called Gaz. He would know what to do. It was just after 6am. Gaz answered.

"Roy's been captured" was all I could say.

"Ok, keep calm," said Gaz, "Just carry on as normal. I'll take care of a few things here". Then he hung up.

Sue said that the police were from Romford CID and had left a number for her. She said she would call it at 9.00am and then she would go to her mum's. Would I look after the shop and run everything? Of course I would.

The cash and jewellery were kept hidden under the cold meat counter. There was two thousand pounds in cash and some odds and sods of jewellery. Everything in the garage was gone. It was mainly cases of wine that had come in yesterday which were supposed to go to Mr. Patel later that day. I called Mr. Patels cash and carry, but no one had seen him that day and nobody seemed to know where he was. Now I was getting nervous.

I opened the shop as normal at 08.00. The other butcher turned up and I explained that Roy had a family emergency and would be away for a few days. This was not unusual as Roy was quite often away from the shop. Then I got a call from one of the cousins, Teddy.

"I hear Roy's been captured, act normal and keep your mouth shut."

That's all he said. There wasn't any stress in his voice, just a professional manner; I supposed he'd been through this many times.

During the day a couple of delivery drivers came in and said they had some stuff, I told them not to come in for a while. "The Butcher's been captured."

They soon got the message and fucked off.

Sue called the CID. "Roy's being held in Hertfordshire somewhere. He's been moved from Romford and he's spoken with his solicitor. I can't see him yet. That's all they've said." She started to cry again.

"Ok, be strong, its gonna be ok, you know what Roy's like, he's probably taking freezer orders from the old bill as we speak." We both laughed.

Sue packed a few things, then she and the twins went off to her mum's.

The other Cousin, Danny, called later that day.

"If you can get a message to Roy, tell him to fuck off whatever solicitor he's got. He can use our one. But he can't contact Roy until he gets his permission so get Roy to call me as soon as he can."

I explained to him that Roy had been moved to a place in Hertfordshire. Danny told me that these things were quite common.

"If they come for you Joe, just be strong and keep your mouth shut. You just work in the shop, you're just the butcher boy and you know nothing, understand?"

"Okay."

But really I was shit scared.

Chapter 24

Changes

That Monday was the most hectic of days. Calls were coming in fast and furious as the word got round about Roy. Colin was on the phone about five times that day. They'd decided to stop printing the luncheon vouchers for a while. Colin, like me, had got rid of everything that was in his house. Roy's older brother Frank came into the shop and asked if there was anything I needed. We decided that it should be business as usual and to try not to let too many people know about Roy's arrest.

I ended up having to tell the guys in the shop the truth. They'd guessed as much. I made them promise not to mention it to any of the customers.

I was glad we closed at 1.00pm on Mondays. I didn't go straight home. I went to the pub and had a few beers. I needed to think. I was still convinced that I would be taken away by the police. Even if I wasn't arrested, surely, I thought, they would want to question me?

By the third pint I was beginning to see things a bit clearer. What exactly did they have? So far, they would have about fifty cases of stolen wine. That's all that was in the garage as far as I could remember. So they would charge Roy with handling stolen goods, and if it was only the wine that they were charging him with, it was his first offence, so maybe he'd get a suspended sentence.

By the time I got home, I had convinced myself that it wasn't too bad. I suddenly realised why the Cousins and Gaz kept saying we should all keep our mouths shut. If no one said anything then they didn't have much on Roy. Just the wine.

I slept a bit more comfortably that night.

I was up and in work by 6.30am the next day. There was no one in the flat; Sue had obviously spent the night at her parents. Gaz came in about 6.45am.

"Morning mate, how you doing. Any news?"

"Nothing yet Gaz, no one's been able to see him yet, Sue might know something a bit later."

"Okay, here's the deal. If they come for you, you know nothing, okay, nothing. You are just the boy here. You just cut up meat, you know nothing about any deals and most importantly you know about me."

There was a slight menace in his voice and his words came across as a bit of a threat. Roy had taught me well. He always said when you get threatened, always come back strong.

"What do you think I am Gaz, some kind of cunt? Of course I know nothing; I just cut up fucking meat. I'm just a butcher for fuck's sake!"

"Good boy." Gaz gave me a smile and a wink, then left the shop.

I was quite proud of myself. I had stood up strong. I went back to work.

At about 9.30am a stranger came in, a tall slim guy in his late thirties. Dark hair, hadn't shaved for a couple of days so he had a bit of a scruffy look about him. I went to serve him.

"Morning guv, what you after?"

"A mate of mine told me you had a few cases of wine going cheap."

"Wine? This is a butcher's shop mate. You need the off license up the road."

"No, I want some wine! You know, cheap, I could do with a couple of cases. He also said that you got other bits and pieces from time to time. Got anything in the shop now?"

"Look mate, no idea what you're talking about, we just sell meat here. Whoever your mate is, he's winding you up."

The guy shrugged and left. He crossed the road and got into a silver car. There was another guy in the car. Definitely old bill. What the fuck were they playing at? Did they really expect me to be that naïve?

Mr. Patel called. "How's Roy doing? I've just heard the news."

"Not sure, no one's been allowed to see him yet, but you know what he's like, he'll be Okay. How about you?"

"Yeah, everything's Okay, business as usual. If you need anything just let me know."

"Cheers mate."

So it looked like it was only Roy that had been captured. This was good news. As long as Roy said nothing everything should be fine.

Roy pleads not guilty to the wine, just say's he bought it cheap from a driver he's never met before. Didn't know it was knocked off. It's for a large family party that's coming up. It could just even be a big fine.

I saw Sue later that day. She said that she had been allowed to speak with Roy and he was being held at St Albans police station. He was being charged for handling stolen goods and had a good solicitor. He said to thank the Cousins for their offer but he's Okay with the solicitor he's got. She said he sounded calm and in control, although he'd had almost no sleep for over thirty six hours. He was to appear before magistrates in the morning and he was going to plead not guilty.

I told her this was all good news. He'd be charged, appear before magistrates, get bail and be home before the day was out. She started crying again. This was a mixture of emotions: sadness because Roy wasn't there, but also a sense of relief that it could all be over soon.

I called Gaz and told him the news.

"Brilliant news mate, he pleads not guilty, gets bail, comes home and then we work out his story with a good brief. Then we all go down the pub and get pissed. I'll tell the Cousins. Well done mate, you did well."

Yep, it was looking like it would soon be over.

Roy appeared before the magistrates the next day and he pleaded not guilty to handling stolen goods. But for some reason bail was refused, and Roy was taken to Bedford prison on remand. We were all in shock. Sue had driven to the magistrate's court thinking she would be bringing Roy home. When she got back to the shop she was in bits. I think she must have cried all the way back.

"They refused bail on the grounds that they think he may offend again before it goes to trial; they're treating him like he's some kind of Mister big."

This wasn't good news; perhaps they had more on Roy than we thought.

I had to give Gaz and the Cousins the bad news. They weren't as confident this time.

I remember Gaz's reaction. He kept saying "That's not right, that's definitely not right. There has to be something else. Something we don't know about."

Sue went back to her Mum's and I got on with running the shop. I was now doing all the ordering and paying all the wages. It was like it was my business. Roy had taught me well, and it all came easily.

After a week, Sue was told she could see Roy in Bedford prison; she didn't want to go on her own but I couldn't go as I was running the shop, so my dad took her.

Sue and Roy had an hour together.

Roy was held on remand for another three weeks. Then out of the blue, he was granted bail and was coming home. Once again this all happened very quickly. One minute he was in prison, the next he was on his way home. Sue said it was because his solicitor had worked hard for his release and convinced the old bill that Roy wasn't a threat.

Roy came home on a Friday night. I saw him for the first time when I got into the shop on the Saturday morning. You'd have thought I'd only seen him the day before.

"Morning mate. You okay? Thanks for looking after everything while I was away."

"No problem Roy. Looks like you've lost weight; mind you, you were getting to be a fat fucker."

I never saw the first egg as it hit me, or the second. Yep, Roy was back.

But things would never be the same again.

Chapter 25

Goodbye

Roy called Gaz, the Cousins, and Colin. He told them they should all stay away from the shop for a while. He was convinced that he and the shop were being watched. He called them from the public phone box across the street.

"Don't contact me for a while. They're all over me. I'll contact you when everything's died down a bit."

Roy used the call box from then on. He told me that he didn't trust the phone in the shop in case the old bill were listening in. It all made sense to me. Every time the shop phone rang Roy would stop whatever he was doing and run to answer it. He would speak in a whisper so that no one could overhear him. There were lots of these phone calls in the first few weeks after Roy was released. I never knew who he was talking to. I assumed it was his solicitor.

The business was slow, as I said before; the Fords strike lasted for over a month and almost into November. Inflation was running at fifteen percent, and everyone was worried about job security. This meant that Christmas might not be as good as it had been in previous years.

Christmas was exactly that - quiet. Normally at the close of business on Christmas Eve we were all tired but buzzing. It was always a mad adrenaline fuelled day. Every year we would sell out of everything. But this year was different. We had at least fifty turkeys and various rolls of beef and legs of pork still sitting in the window going nowhere. Roy was gutted.

"That's my fucking profit sitting in that window."

We shut up shop and drove to Ridley Road market in Bethnal Green and started selling them out of the back of the transit. We got rid of all of them but for hardly any money. By the time Roy paid me and the others he had hardly any cash left for himself. A few months earlier and he would have laughed it off. But there were no more deals going on so no extra cash coming in.

Roy had changed. No longer was he the larger than life character that everyone loved, the cheeky chappy, the loveable rogue. Now he was quieter, more cautious, more subdued. He seemed to have aged overnight. I just thought that being in prison and being away from Sue and the twins for those few weeks had taken its toll, physically and mentally.

January came and still there was no date set for Roy's trial. He would disappear for hours on end. He never told me where he was going, which was totally out of character.

Gaz started coming back into the shop in March and so did the cousins. I thought the four of them were back to their old ways. But now it was different, now Roy didn't include me. Nothing came into the shop anymore. Everything went straight to Mr. Patel or on to another contact. It was as if Roy was trying to keep his distance from what was going on and in the process trying to protect me. This went on for months. I also noticed that Roy's close family stopped coming in. I hadn't seen Frank for months or any other members of the family.

Just before Easter in April 1977 we closed the shop for half day as we always did on a Thursday.

"Come for a pint Joe, I want to have a word."

We went to our local pub. Roy bought two pints and two whisky chasers.

I laughed at him.

"Well it's definitely not my birthday and I don't think it's yours so what we celebrating?"

He smiled. But it was a nervous smile.

"I'm gonna call it a day soon mate. Me and Sue are looking at some properties down near Bournemouth. I've got a few bob tucked away and we want to make a fresh start somewhere different. Do you want to rent the shop from me?"

I was stunned.

"What? What do you mean, call it a day, how you gonna live in fucking Bournemouth? It's full of old people waiting to die."

"I want to get away from what I'm doing, you know, with Gaz and the Cousins. I'll never be able to do that if I stay here. It's not fair on Sue and the kids."

"How soon?"

"In a couple of months, maybe sooner, but when we decide to go, it'll be quick. Like one day I'll be there and the next day gone, so you need to be ready if you decide to take this on board."

"Yeah but taking over the shop. Fuck, that's a big job."

Now his big smile returned and he suddenly became the old Roy again.

"Bollocks, you've been running the fucking place for the past two years!"

We both laughed, shook hands and agreed a figure of seventy five pounds per week for the rent. Roy said that he would show me anything that he thought I didn't know between now and when he left.

Roy made me promise one thing. I wouldn't tell anyone, especially Gaz and the Cousins. I promised. I never even told my mum and dad.

The next couple of months were manic, the phone in the shop was constantly ringing and Roy was being very secretive about everything. They were planning something, I knew it. Perhaps Roy was going to do one last big job then call it a day and he was keeping me out of it in case it all went pear shaped.

Yeah that's what it was. What else could it be?

Then in June, without any warning, it happened. Just four days after the Silver Jubilee celebrations, Roy closed the shop on Saturday as usual and we went across to the pub.

"Sue and I are leaving tomorrow mate, we've found a new place in Ferndale near Bournemouth. From Monday it's all yours."

"Jesus Roy, that quick? No leaving do, no saying goodbye to everyone? What shall I tell the punters?"

"Look, don't worry, I'll still keep in touch, phone you a couple of times a week to make sure everything's okay. Pay the rent money direct to my solicitor in St Albans, he's gonna look after all the paperwork. Just keep doing what you've been doing for a long time, you'll earn some good money. I know things are a bit quiet at the moment but it'll pick up. Even now you'll clear a few hundred quid a week."

"How long for Roy? I mean how long before you decide to sell it?"

"I don't know, six months or so, see what you think. If you decide you want to buy it and you can raise a bit of money, it's yours. We're mates, we'll work something out."

"What about Gaz and all the others, what shall I tell them?"

"Listen, just say that me and Sue have found a new house and we had to move quickly or we'd lose it. Tell them I'll be in touch in the next couple of weeks, once we've sorted ourselves out."

We had a couple of beers, shook hands and then went back to the shop. Roy gave me the number of his solicitor in St Albans and said that he would be in touch the following week. But he didn't give me any details about how to contact him or Sue. Roy said that they were moving to a brand new house in a new street that didn't even have a name yet. There wasn't even a phone there yet. But he assured me he would give me a call as soon as possible.

I walked out of the shop, wondering if I would ever see Roy again. Something inside me knew that something was wrong, but I couldn't work out what it was.

As I walked away the radio was playing "Don't Leave Me This Way" by Harold Melvin. I remember smiling and thinking, how fucking appropriate.

I didn't realise then but it would be a very long time before I saw Roy again. In fact, almost a lifetime.

Chapter 26

The Visit

So on Monday 13th June 1977, at the tender age of nineteen, I had my own butchers shop. You'd think I would have been pleased, but it just wasn't the same without Roy. However, business did pick up. I changed the sign outside. It now said "Joes Joint".I started doing things a bit differently to how Roy had done them. I started cooking whole chickens and selling them, making three more flavours of sausages, two more types of burgers, and a lot more cold meats. It seemed to work - takings went up by twenty per-cent.

I paid my rent each week, by cheque, to Roy's solicitor in St Albans. Roy called a couple of times a week for the first month, asking how things were going and all in all it seemed to be working out okay. But, to be honest, I missed Roy. We'd spent virtually every day together for the past five years. It was like having a close brother that suddenly emigrates to Australia.

I had a couple of visits from Gaz who was worried about Roy's sudden departure, but I told him what Roy had told me about having to move quick or they would lose their new house, and he seemed to accept it. So did the Cousins. But they were all concerned that he had left no forwarding address or phone number. I explained that their new house was indeed just that, brand spanking new, not even a road name yet. But Roy assured me that he would contact them in the next couple of weeks.

Then it all kicked off.

The first to go was Trevor. Trevor was captured on his way home from work after doing his night shift at the record warehouse. His house was raided and they found a few thousand records and tapes. Meads records and tapes was raided and closed. It never opened again.

Colin was next. His home was raided at dawn on Tuesday 16th August (in fact on the same day that Elvis died), and large quantities of counterfeit luncheon vouchers were seized. A small lock up in Bow was raided, containing a printing press and over half a million pounds worth of luncheon vouchers.

Then, old Ken. Ken's little corner shop was raided the same day. Vouchers and coupons were seized along with thousands of pounds worth of groceries.

My phone never stopped ringing that Tuesday. Everyone wanted to get hold of Roy, asking where was he, had he been captured again, who else did I know, that had been pulled in? All questions I couldn't answer. I called Roy's solicitor. He wouldn't take my call. He was either on the phone, in court or with clients.

Once again I began to think that I would be next. I went home that night convinced that Roy had been captured and that my time was up. But nothing.

The next day I was up and at the shop by 5.20am. I was anxious to find out if there was any more news. I half expected there to be a Police car outside waiting for me. But instead, Gaz was parked up outside. He was obviously waiting for me to open up. But he wasn't alone. He had two very sinister looking guys with him. I'd never seen them before.

All three of them followed me into the shop.

"Morning Gaz. You're early, what's happening?"

" I was hoping you could tell me, Joe."

"Only the same as yesterday Gaz, Colin and a few others were all captured, that's all I know."

"And Roy, what about Roy?"

"No idea, can't get hold of him. He's not called in for days, maybe he's been done as well."

"Did you speak with his solicitor?"

"No, the fucker was busy all day, didn't answer my calls."

I could tell by his face that he was losing his temper. He raised his voice.

"Now look here Joe, this is serious, very serious. People are falling like fucking flies, the old bill know things, things they shouldn't know, things they can't possibly know, but they fucking do know. Which means that someone's talking. When we find out who it is, we'll fucking do em. Understand?"

There was real menace in his voice. One of the guys with him picked up one of the big steak knives and started throwing it from one hand to the other.

"Well I can tell you it ain't me Gaz. You do know that. Don't you?"

"Lucky for you, I *know* it's not you, but Roy, I'm not so sure. Roy goes missing and then everyone gets captured. Doesn't look good does it?"

"No way, Gaz, not Roy, he wouldn't grass. No way."

"Well all I'm saying is, it don't look good. So if he calls you, you fucking let me know straightaway, you understand Joe, straightaway. You call me the fucking minute you hear from him, and you tell him to fucking come and see me. We need to straighten this out."

I tried not to show it, but I was petrified. I knew Gaz and I knew what he was capable of. I was just glad that he didn't think I was involved. But Roy, surely not Roy?

"Okay Gaz, message understood. Have you heard from the Cousins? What do they think?"

"They were captured at four o'clock this morning."

"Fuck!"

Gaz and his two silent thugs left the shop. I went to the sink and threw up.

What the fuck was going on?

I started to work but couldn't concentrate. I was wondering where the fuck Roy was. I actually hoped he'd been arrested.

Just after 10.00am the phone rang. It was Roy.

"Morning mate, everything okay?"

He sounded as calm as a cucumber. I was wound up so tight that I started shouting down the phone.

"Okay? You joking? No it's fucking not okay. Everyone's been captured, Colin, Ken, the Cousins, Trevor. All fucking taken, all of them. Where the fuck are you?"

"Calm down, calm down. What's been said?"

"Gaz was here this morning. He ain't happy, he thinks you're a fucking grass."

"Bollocks, listen, tell Gaz it's nothing to do with me."

"No way, you fucking tell him. He wants you to get in contact straightaway!"

"Okay, okay. Calm down. I'll call him later today. He'll be fine. Look I've got to go. I'll call back later."

Roy hung up.

I called Gaz just like I told him I would.

"Gaz, it's Joe. I just spoke to Roy, he's going to call you later today. He said don't worry it's nothing to do with him."

"Thank fuck for that. Okay, thanks for letting me know. I'll speak with Roy and arrange a meet. We need to get to the bottom of this and find out who this fucking grass is."

I was relieved. Roy and Gaz would talk. They'd work things out and maybe we could get some answers.

But Roy never did call Gaz, or he was too late. Either way it didn't matter.

Later that day Gaz was arrested along with another twenty eight people in East London. Including Mr. Patel.

If I thought I was scared before, now I was terrified.

Chapter 27

The Truth At Last

Then everything went quiet. There were no more calls from Roy. I heard from one or two sources that the Cousins, Colin and Gaz were being held on remand. They had been charged with various offences and no bail had been granted in case they fled the country. I had no idea whether Roy was being held as well.

I had no way of contacting Sue either, no phone number, no address. Roy's solicitor was hard work. He kept saying he couldn't discuss anything to do with Roy apart from business related to the shop. I paid him my rent every week but that was the only contact I had with him.

Roy's brother Frank had moved from his house in East Ham and no one seemed to know where he had moved to, so I couldn't ask him what was going on.

For the next few months there was no contact, no word, nothing.

Then I got a call from Roy's solicitor. The rental agreement was due for renewal. It was a six month contract. Did I wish to continue for a further six months? I said yes and he invited me to attend a meeting at his office. I asked if Roy would be there. He said he would. A date was fixed for the following week.

I was excited, I hadn't seen Roy for five months, and there were all sorts of rumours about him but nothing was certain. Perhaps now I would get a chance to find out what was going on. It was unthinkable that Roy was a grass. I thought that he was just keeping quiet, keeping his head down, not wanting to get involved. He had his own case to think about for Christ's sake. It also crossed my mind that there might be another reason. Maybe all the worry has taken its toll. Maybe he'd been ill, mentally ill. But all being well I would find out at the meeting in St. Albans.

I went to the solicitors the following week. The meeting was planned for 4.30pm. I arrived there early and went for a couple of pints first. When I entered the solicitors' office, there was no Roy. Just the solicitor sitting there.

"Where's Roy?"

"He couldn't make it, but he's given me authorisation to act on his behalf."

"But you said he would be here!"

I realised I was shouting. A wave of emotions swept through me. I was upset, angry, confused. I wanted to see Roy. He was my best mate. I missed him. Where the fuck was he?

"Please calm down and take a seat. Mr. Marshall isn't well enough to attend the meeting today. But he has assured me that he will contact you in the next few days."

This confirmed what I had thought earlier. Maybe Roy was ill after all.

We did the deal. Same rent as before, for another six months, and after this we would look at the possibility of me buying the shop. The solicitor said that Roy had agreed to be very generous with the price and would even help me raise the funds if necessary.

I went back to East Ham with mixed emotions. I was unhappy that I hadn't seen Roy, but happy that he had said he would contact me in a few days. About bloody time, the old bastard, we had a lot to talk about.

It was now November 1977, Christmas was just around the corner and I hadn't heard from Roy since August. I hadn't seen him since June. I missed him, we were about to come up to the busiest time of the year and Roy had always been around at Christmas. He was the one that really ran things at this time of the year. We used to laugh and joke about him never being around, but at Christmas he worked just as hard as everyone else, in fact even harder. I still had my two boys, Dave and Fred, who helped out. Freddy had come in everyday throughout the school holidays, Davey came in on Saturdays and also after school during the week. They could both draw a chicken, skin a rabbit and make mince and sausages. But they didn't want to be butchers. They didn't have the drive that I had at their age. They were now both sixteen. The part timer was now almost full time, the only days he didn't work were the half days, Mondays and Thursdays. So I had enough staff, I just didn't have Roy.

I kept thinking about what the Solicitor had said, that Roy would be in touch. But when?

November and December came and went. Christmas was frantic. I ordered the Turkeys from the same farmer that Roy used and sold all two hundred of them. Every regular customer was given a glass of whisky or sherry and Christmas Eve was like one big family party. I made just over two grand. A huge amount of money for a nineteen year old.

I turned twenty at the end of January 1978. There was still no word from Roy. Old Ken had pleaded guilty to the coupon scam and was awaiting a trial date. He had been given bail but kept his distance from me and the shop. Mr. Patel was also charged with fraud and handling stolen goods, and he was also given bail. But Gaz, Colin and the Cousins were all being held on remand awaiting trial. Because of the luncheon vouchers they were being treated as though they had been printing currency. The old tax man takes a very dim view of that.

Occasionally a driver would come in and say he had this or that but I would send him on his way. I'd tell him not to come back and spread the word to all the other drivers. No one came in now.

But trade was good.

The months flew by. Everyone was talking about somebody called the Yorkshire Ripper, bodies were found in parts of Yorkshire and also in Manchester, a man hunt was under way. This meant nothing to me of course -all I wanted was an answer to what was going on in the bloody East London of London. There was still no call from Roy. Still no word from Gaz, Colin or the Cousins, they were all still banged up.

On Tuesday 11th July 1978, I went to Smithfield Market to buy some meat. I got there around 04.30am. I bought what I needed and drove back to the shop. I arrived back at the shop at around 06.15am.

I started to unload the meat when a regular lady customer saw me and shouted out from across the street. "Buy the Daily Mirror, buy the Daily Mirror!"

I finished unloading and went next door to the paper shop. That's when I saw it, that's when everything fell into place, that's when all the questions were answered.

The headline ran: "ARMED POLICE GUARD SUPERGRASS AFTER 70 ARRESTS", "Squealer hides for his life!" The article said "If this man went back to East London, he would be dead within a day."

Yes, they were talking about Roy.

Chapter 28

Moving On

The phone was ringing, it was just before 6.30am and the bloody phone was ringing. I was trying to take it all in. I read the front page about six times, every bloody word. They mentioned Roy and the butchers shop. They didn't give the address of the shop, thank fuck, just that he used to have a butchers shop in East London.

They were saying he was the biggest supergrass of all time. Even bigger than Bertie Smalls, and he was a bloody household name in the East End, a bloody bogie man. Everyone hated Bertie Smalls! A grass was someone you hated, despised, they were lower than low. Now Roy was the biggest grass of all time.

I wasn't sure how I felt about it. This was Roy after all, my best mate, he was like a brother to me. Yet I should hate him for what he'd done. He'd sold everyone down the bloody swanny river just to save his own arse. Everyone we'd called mates, everyone who was part of the "firm", was going to be banged up because of Roy. Fuck, even me, they might still come for me.

The phone was still ringing, I ignored it. I went back to the paper shop and bought a copy of every daily paper. It was in the Mail, Express and Sun. Not quite the front page as it was in the Mirror, but still mentioned in all of them. Fuck.

The phone was still ringing. This time I answered it. It was my Mum.

"We've just read the papers. Is everything okay at the shop?"

"Yes Mum. It's fine."

"Maybe you should close up for now. What if there's trouble, what if some nasty people decide that they want revenge and take it out on you, or attack the shop?"

"Mum, it's fine, honest. First sign of trouble and I'll close. I promise."

While I was speaking with Mum, my Dad walked into the shop.

"I'm going Mum, Dads just walked in."

I hung up. As big and hard as I thought I was, my eyes began to fill up. God was I pleased to see the old man.

"I've taken a few days off work, thought you could do with some help."

For the first time in years I gave my dad a big hug.

"Thanks dad."

As you would expect the day was manic. Everyone wanted to know what was going on. Customers we hadn't seen in years suddenly decided to come in and buy something, and of course they mentioned Roy.

There wasn't much I could tell them. I hadn't seen Roy for over a year, and I hadn't spoken to him for god knows how long.

The phone rang around midday, Dad answered it. "It's for you Joe, some bloke about a freezer order."

I took the call.

"Morning mate, what can I do for you?"

"Is that the boy? The butcher boy?"

I didn't recognise the voice, but as soon as he mentioned butcher boy, I knew it must be something to do with Roy.

"Yeah mate, what's up?"

"I'm a friend of a couple of people you know. They're extremely unhappy with their current situation. So if you hear of the whereabouts of a certain person you let me know, yeah?"

He gave me a number. I wrote it down. Then he hung up.

He was obviously talking about the Cousins.

I had been expecting something. I wasn't sure what I had been expecting, but I was expecting something. I got back to work, but didn't mention it to Dad. There wasn't much more I could do, I couldn't go to the old bill.

It did make me think though. Maybe staying in the shop wasn't such a good idea. I closed the shop at 6.00pm as usual, and Dad and I went home.

I sat down with them and told them that I'd decided not to buy the shop afterall. I would work through the next few months but then close up. Staying in the shop wasn't such a great idea. They were both relieved.

I called the solicitor the next morning and gave him the news. He said he would make the necessary arrangements. An hour later the phone rang.

"Hello you old bastard!"

It was Roy. Even though I should have hated him for what he'd done, just hearing his voice made me smile.

"Fuck me, the last person in the world I was expecting, what's it like to be the most hated person in Britain?"

We both laughed.

"Seriously Joe, don't believe everything you read in the papers. There'll be a lot more in the next few days and some of it is total bollocks. I understand why you want to get out of the shop. I understand. It's fine with me. I'll try to call again but they've got me on a very tight leash. If they knew I was calling you now they would go mad."

Then he hung up, no goodbye, he just put the phone down. I guessed he had to go quickly and by "they" he meant the old bill.

He was right; he was in the papers a lot. A few weeks later he was on the front page of the Daily Mirror again. This time his information had led to the arrest of a gang who had been holding up security vans and cutting their way in with a chain saw!

But he never called again.

It took time for everything to get sorted out legally but the end was inevitable.

Roy would now have to stand up in court and give evidence against people he had once been friends with.

The trial was held in secret without any publicity. The Police were concerned that if word got out that Roy was at court everyday, he might become a target. I didn't know what was happening until I picked up the newspaper one day and saw a small section on page four of the Sun.

The Cousins got ten years each. Colin and Gaz both got seven.

Roy had grassed everyone apart from me, from delivery drivers to hardened criminals. For his help he was given an eighteen month sentence suspended for two years. He would never see prison.

I closed the shop at the end of 1978, still only twenty. A lot had happened in the past six years, and though I was still a kid, I was now also very much a man.

Chapter 29

New Challenges

I got a job at a meat wholesalers in Walthamstow, East London. I was supplying shops just like Roy's. They also had a place in Smithfield Market. I started early (5.00am) and was always finished by midday; I did three days in Walthamstow and two at Smithfield.

I was called the Assistant Sales Manager, but really I was a glorified checker.

I checked things in and I checked things out. It was easy, and of course having been taught by Roy I soon noticed that here was a way of earning lots of money. This would be the best job in the world.

I was in charge of checking things onto the Lorries, and of course, I knew that all the drivers were looking for a few "extras". I quickly became very popular with all seven delivery drivers.

Everything was unionised back then, and everyone had to do their own job. A driver was a driver, he wasn't allowed to pick his own orders, that was the job of the porter. I told the porters what orders were needed, they went into the large chillers and freezers and got the orders ready then took them to be weighed and checked. Once this had been done they were taken to the lorry where the order was loaded on board by the driver. My job was to check and weigh everything before it was loaded.

For example, order number one is for three pigs, twelve lambs, three shins of beef, two boxes of lamb's liver and a pack of pig's kidneys. I give the porter the list, he goes and gets it, he puts the various items onto the scale, I check the weight of each item and write out a ticket (invoice) for it. Easy.

However, if you are a certain way inclined, out of just this one order we would all make good money. It was wide open for abuse and god did we abuse it.

Everyone wanted a piece of the action, the drivers, the porters and of course the customers.

The orders came in by telephone. Part of my job was to take the telephone calls as they came in. Very quickly I knew every butcher by their first name and soon got to know the ones who were "up for it".

So for the same order, I would weigh the three pigs. The real weight might be two hundred and eighty pounds , but I would write out a ticket for two hundred and twenty, thus saving the customer sixty pounds in weight. I would also pretend not to notice as another three pigs and four lambs were loaded onto the vehicle by the porter without being weighed. The driver would sell these "extras" to one of his "regulars". Every driver, every day had something "extra" on board. It suddenly dawned on me that this was exactly how Roy had started out. I wasn't sure if that was a good thing or not.

Friday's were pay out day. I made a list during the week of the "extras" that each driver had then we all met in the pub at midday where the drivers gave me and the porters our share. After that I would drive round to four or five of my customers and collect the money they owed me. Once again I was raking it in. Roy had been a great teacher.

It lasted eighteen months before I was suddenly called into the office and told that I wasn't needed anymore. No big deal, I would find another job quickly, and surely, every job had a scam attached to it.

Roy's shop was sold to a husband and wife team who had a dream of becoming shopkeepers. They had no idea about butchery. They approached me and asked if I would consider coming back part time, perhaps a couple of afternoons a week to cut the meat up so all they then had to do was sell it. I knew it wouldn't work but they offered me good money so I couldn't refuse.

I got another job in the market and ran the same scam but on a much smaller scale. I finished by midday and then went back to the old shop to do some cutting and packing for a few hours.

You'd have thought that I'd have been happy being back in the shop, but there were too many memories. Every time I walked in I expected to hear his voice or his laugh. I missed him and the shop made me realise just how much I missed him. So after four months I quit. I left the shop that day and never set foot in it again.

Smithfield Market had a huge crash in 1979 with a couple of the big players going bust; the knock on effect was that a lot of the smaller wholesalers also went under. I turned up for work one Monday morning and was told that I, along with six or seven others, were no longer needed. There was no more work in Smithfield.

For the next fifteen years I did worked various jobs. I never seemed to be able to settle anywhere for more than a year or so. I missed the shop, I missed the banter - in a nutshell I missed my mate Roy.

I had no idea where he was, what he was doing, how his life was. I had so many unanswered questions. He even entered my dreams at night. Every night. He had been a big influence on me from such an early age; he had moulded me into the person that I had become.

 I wondered whether I would I ever see him again.

Chapter 30

The Reunion

By 1996 I had long left the meat trade. The industry had changed so much in twenty years that it no longer held any attraction for me. Supermarkets were dominating the food market and small independent Butcher's shops were no longer able to make a profit and were closing down everywhere.

Roy's old shop was now an Indian restaurant and where there was once three shops in the small precinct there were now none. A trade that I loved was now just a fading memory.

I was now in the transport industry and running a courier company just behind Kings Cross station in central London. I finished work for the day and began the long drive home to Essex. The traffic was a nightmare. I was driving through Bow and decided to let the traffic die down. I stopped at a pub I had never been in before. It was a typical East End pub, the sort of pub that when a stranger walks in the music stops and everyone looks at you, especially if you're wearing a suit. I was wearing a suit. I stopped just inside the door, smiled and decided to break the ice.

"It's okay, I'm not the old bill, I'm just getting out of this fucking traffic."

A few people laughed and got on with what they were doing before.

Then I heard a familiar voice from behind the bar. "Fuck me, look who it is. Hello stranger."

It was Roy's brother Frank.

We did the man hug thing, and then we started talking. I hadn't seen him in almost twenty years. We talked all evening about the old days. The one thing he made quite clear at the very start of our long talk was that he couldn't say anything about Roy. Apart from saying that he and Sue were fine and so were the twins. He emphasised that that was all he could tell me.

I was disappointed, but I understood. After almost twenty years Roy still had to be careful.

I left the car at Frank's pub that night and went home extremely pissed.

Over the next few years, Frank and I became firm friends, best friends in fact. He was so much like Roy, and I enjoyed being with him. It was the same for him. He couldn't see his younger brother very often but being with me reminded him of Roy. It worked both ways. I popped in to Franks's pub about twice a week, either on my way home or to watch a football match. Any excuse really. Whenever we met he would always start the conversation with, "Roy's fine, before you ask."

In 2004 Frank gave me some bad news. Roy had cancer and was having chemotherapy; he wouldn't say anymore about it, only that Roy was very ill. I was gutted. I had always thought he was bigger than life itself, indestructible.

In September 2004 I was at work when I got a call. It was Frank. He said to come to the pub today around 1.00pm if I could. He didn't say why, but I guessed it was important. So I took the rest of the day off.

When I got to the pub, Frank was waiting with his coat on.

"Don't sit down, get in your car and follow me. Someone wants to see you."

He smiled and gave me a wink.

Suddenly I was like a little kid again waiting to see Father Christmas. I knew I was going to see Roy again, twenty eight years after I last saw him.

We left the pub in Bow and drove down the M11. We came off at Harlow and drove to a travel lodge just outside Harlow town. We parked the cars and walked in to the bar of the hotel.

Sitting in a chair in the corner by the bar was a bald, frail, grey faced man. He stood up and said, "Hello you old bastard."

It was Roy. He had changed so much but his voice was just the same. We put our arms around each other and I realised he was just skin and bone. This once big, powerful, larger than life character was a shadow of his former self. He stood back and took a long look at me.

"Look at the fucking size of you, no longer the boy, a grown man, what, forty now?"

"Forty six mate."

"Fuck, twenty eight years, twenty eight fucking years!"

We sat in the bar for hours; Frank left us so we could catch up. We talked about everything, and I mean everything. He'd been all over the world. Dubai, Bahrain, New Zealand, Switzerland. But he had now settled back in the UK.

He knew he was dying, he even laughed about it. He'd even picked out the songs for his funeral.

At about 7.00pm he looked at his watch and said, "I better go." We hugged again and that's when he broke down.

"I am so sorry mate, so fucking sorry, I screwed my life up, I couldn't bear to fuck yours up as well. That's why I couldn't get in touch, I couldn't chance it. Forgive me?"

He was in tears and now I was. Two grown men hugging in a bar and crying their eyes out.

"Of course I forgive you, you old bastard."

We parted and each got into our cars. I never saw him again.

Roy died six weeks later, at the age of fifty six. He had spent almost thirty years having to pretend to be another person. I didn't go to the funeral, I couldn't bear to. We had already said our goodbyes.

I am now fifty four, and I have been many things in my life. But deep down I think I'm still just an east end butcher boy.

THE END

Printed in Great Britain
by Amazon

84974881R10092